STRUCTURED

Writing

Using Inspiration Software to Teach Paragraph Development

Charles Haynes
Kathleen McMurdo

International Society for Technology in Education
EUGENE, OREGON

Structured Writing
Using Inspiration software to teach paragraph development
Charles Haynes and Kathleen McMurdo

Director of Publishing
Jean Marie Hall

Acquisitions Editors
Anita McAnear
Mathew Manweller

Book Publishing Project Manager
Tracy Cozzens

Data and Communications Manager
Diannah Anavir

Copy Editor
Steve Cozzens

Cover Design
Katherine Getta

Layout and Production
Tracy Cozzens

International Society for Technology in Education (ISTE)
480 Charnelton Street
Eugene, OR 97401-2626
Order Desk: 800.336.5191
Order Fax: 541.302.3778
Customer Service: orders@iste.org
Books and Courseware: books@iste.org
Permissions: permissions@iste.org
World Wide Web: www.iste.org

First Edition
ISBN 1-56484-171-5

About ISTE

The International Society for Technology in Education (ISTE) is a nonprofit professional organization with a worldwide membership of leaders in educational technology. We are dedicated to promoting appropriate uses of information technology to support and improve learning, teaching, and administration in PK–12 education and teacher education. As part of that mission, ISTE provides high-quality and timely information, services, and materials, such as this book.

The ISTE Publishing Department works with experienced educators to develop and produce classroom-tested books and courseware. We look for content that emphasizes the use of technology where it can make a difference—making the teacher's job easier; saving time; motivating students; helping students who have unique learning styles, abilities, or backgrounds; and creating learning environments that would be impossible without technology. We believe technology can improve the effectiveness of teaching while making learning exciting and fun.

Every manuscript and product we select for publication is peer reviewed and professionally edited. While we take pride in our publications, we also recognize the difficulties of maintaining quality while keeping on top of the latest technologies and research. Please let us know which products you would find helpful. We value your feedback on this book and other ISTE products. E-mail us at **books@iste.org**.

ISTE is home of the National Educational Technology Standards (NETS) Project, the National Educational Computing Conference (NECC), and the National Center for Preparing Tomorrow's Teachers to Use Technology (NCPT[3]). To learn more about NETS or request a print catalog, visit our Web site at **www.iste.org**, which provides:

- Current educational technology standards for K–12 student and teacher education
- A bookstore with online ordering and membership discount options
- *Learning & Leading with Technology* magazine and the *Journal of Research on Technology in Education*
- *ISTE Update,* online membership newsletter
- Teacher resources
- Discussion groups
- Professional development services, including national conference information
- Research projects
- Member services

About the Authors

Charles Haynes is the technology coordinator and assistive technology instructor at Chartwell School, a special day school for children ages 7 through 14 who are challenged with dyslexia and related learning disabilities. He has worked as a teacher at Chartwell for the past nine years. He has been a presenter at conferences on the topics of assistive technology and Structured Writing. These conferences include the International Dyslexia Association, the Learning Disabilities Association, Computer Using Educators (CUE), and Technology, Reading and Learning Difficulties (TRLD).

Mr. Haynes has a bachelor of science degree from Indiana State University, a master of science degree in engineering from Rose Polytechnic Institute, and a master of arts degree in special education with a learning handicapped specialty from Chapman University. He has a California Multi-Subject Credential, Special Education Credential, and Resource Specialist Certification.

Kathleen McMurdo is a special education instructor at Chartwell School, a special day school for children ages 7 through 14 who are challenged with dyslexia and related learning disabilities. She has worked as a teacher at Chartwell School for the past eleven years where she collaborated with Charles Haynes, technology coordinator. Together, they developed innovative courses for students and teachers that link direct instruction of the writing process with computer use. From this work, the Structured Writing process has developed.

Ms. McMurdo has presented the Structured Writing techniques extensively at education conferences including the International Dyslexia Association, the Learning Disabilities Association, Computer Using Educators (CUE), and Technology, Reading and Learning Difficulties (TRLD).

Ms. McMurdo received her bachelor of arts degree at San Jose State University and her master of arts degree in special education, specializing in the learning handicapped field, from Chapman University. She has a California Resource Specialist Certification, is Slingerland trained, and teaches the Orton-Gillingham sequence.

Inspired by the struggles of her dyslexic son, an alumnus of Chartwell, Ms. McMurdo completed her degrees as a re-entry student with the intention of working specifically with learning-disabled students. She resides in Carmel, California.

About Write:Outloud

The authors recommend, but do not require, the use of Write:Outloud word-processing software for use in their Structured Writing program. The following is information about the Write:Outloud software program.

Write:OutLoud was originally designed to help students with physical or learning disabilities. However, teachers report that Write:OutLoud motivates all students to write more. The program is so versatile and powerful, it can be used by students through Grade 12. To help increase schools' effectiveness with version control, installation and administration, a network version is available.

Write:OutLoud is a talking word processor. As your students write, the program visually highlights and says the letters, words and sentences on the screen. The program's combined visual and auditory reinforcement gives your students immediate feedback on their writing. By hearing the words and seeing the highlighting, students can self-correct their writing and work independently.

To further develop independent writing skills, Write:OutLoud comes with the Franklin Dictionary with Homonym Checker and the Franklin Spell Checker. Students can consult the on-screen dictionary to check a word's meaning or to find the right word to use. When they have finished writing, the spell checker identifies and corrects spelling errors, including most phonetic spelling errors. Because of these features, as students use Write:OutLoud to improve their writing, they will also see improvements in their reading, spelling and vocabulary.

Write:OutLoud is an easy-to-use tool that students can use throughout the writing process, from brainstorming ideas through first drafts to final polishing, formatting, and printing. To keep students focused on writing instead of how to use a word processor, Write:OutLoud uses on-screen tool icons instead of menu selections.

You may contact Don Johnston at:

Don Johnston
26799 W. Commerce Dr.
Volo, IL 60073
Tel. 800-999-4660
Fax 847-740-7326
www.donjohnston.com

To the Teacher

When faced with that eternal question, "Which came first: the writer or the reader?", we can become as confused as a bunch of chickens looking for their eggs. How can one learn to write effectively without the modeling of other writers gained through years of reading?

This was the dilemma we faced daily in our writing classes of learning disabled students. We observed students' frustration when asked to do tasks with little or no understanding of what was expected. What a terrifying task it is to write those first paragraphs, especially if your experience with the written word has been one of failure.

Working with students to overcome this writing failure, we developed a sequence and structure to our teaching that visually guides students to understand the structure and requirements of their writing. Using the computer allows students to build the structural elements as an independent step and then easily expand and combine these elements into complex paragraphs.

As we discussed these techniques with other teachers, it became apparent that the problems we noted with learning disabled students were shared with many mainstream students. The techniques discussed in this book were initially designed to assist learning disabled students so that they could bridge to a mainstream level. However, the techniques have since proven to be equally effective for teaching mainstream students to write beginning paragraphs and essays.

Our book is a guide for teachers who wish to use these programs to enhance their writing instruction. Our lesson plans are starting points and as teachers we, too, wish to expand our thinking. If, after using these plans, you find new and innovative ways to extend this writing instruction, please share them with us.

Charles Haynes
402 Grove Acre Ave.
Pacific Grove, CA 93950
E-mail: chaynes@chartwell.org

Contents

Introduction

What a terrifying challenge it is to write that first paragraph. For many students, writing sentences, then expanding them into paragraphs, and finally into a multi-paragraph document, is a difficult and frightening process. This is especially true for many students who do not read well or have limited background with the written word. For these students, writing is not a natural means of communication. There are many reasons for this, but it is not our purpose here to discuss those reasons in detail. Our observation of the difficulties students face when given a writing assignment lead us to develop our Structured Writing program using computer templates to guide students through the writing process. This introduction will answer the three questions:

- Why use structured writing?

- Why use computers to teach writing?

- Why use templates to teach writing?

Familiarity with written documents is an important precursor to writing good paragraphs. Students who lack this experience have a difficult time understanding the difference between spoken language and

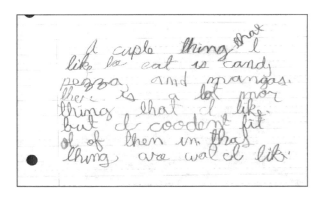

formal writing. Many students with reading difficulties come from situations where reading is not a common activity. Students' reading difficulties are often shared with one, or possibly both, parents. When this is the case, books are not likely to be a form of recreation in the home. Lacking reading experience, students are not comfortable with the syntax of various writing forms. It is the structure of these written forms that students must learn before they can become comfortable expressing themselves in writing.

Many students demonstrate a basic difficulty with organization. They have problems keeping materials in order and find planning tasks difficult. Once planned, a task is often disrupted by many distractions and sidetracks. When starting to write, these disruptions and distractions make it difficult to develop a basic idea through to the creation of a paragraph. We found that by

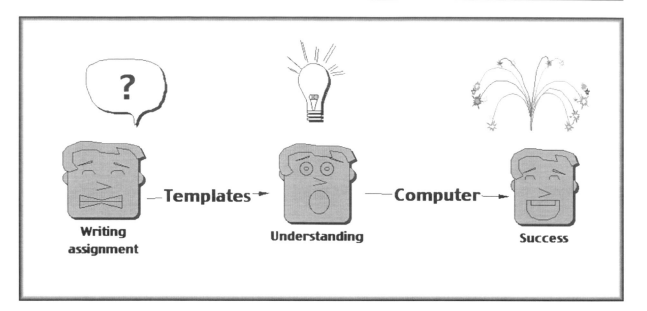

providing the organization through the use of templates and breaking the task into manageable segments using the Structured Writing process, the students were able to overcome this organizational deficit.

Many students continue having difficulty because of their physical or language based disabilities. Students with dysgraphia (the inability to hand write) balk at the many rewrites required for proper editing. Students with spelling problems use minimal vocabulary and frequently have their thought patterns blocked while trying to encode a word. To address these problems, we used the computer. Using the computer,

dysgraphic students were able to allow their thoughts to flow, once reasonable keyboarding skills were acquired. Using a word processing program with a spell checker, thesaurus, and text-to-speech capabilities, students were able to overcome blocks caused by spelling and vocabulary problems. While addressing these basic writing problems, our structured approach to writing instruction evolved.

Why Use Structured Writing?

- **Students do not know where to start when writing.** A lack of background knowledge of written language and confusion generated by the difference in structure between spoken language and formal written language prevents students from getting started. Once started, students do not infer from previous experience what is expected of them in the writing task.

- **Students have difficulty with logical sequencing.** Many students have difficulty remembering linear sequences. The inability to order ideas into a logical sequence is one of the facets of their writing difficulties. Even

Why Use Stuctured Writing?

▶ Students do not know where to start when writing

▶ Students have difficulty with logical sequencing

▶ The visual organizer provides an overall view for the nonlinear thinker

▶ Structure helps students alleviate semantic difficulties

in their spoken language sequencing difficulties are apparent. Without proper planning, writing becomes an impossible task.

- **The visual organizer provides an overall view for the nonlinear thinker.** Teaching to students' learning styles is important. Many students who have difficulty thinking in a linear fashion learn effectively in a global or visual manner. Templates provided in a web form allow students to view the overall structure of each paragraph type visually and provide information showing the differences between those types.

- **Structure helps students alleviate semantic difficulties.** Working in a sentence-by-sentence fashion, with specific guidelines for the content of each sentence, helps students who exhibit semantic difficulties. Without such guides, these students have difficulty giving appropriate meaning to their writing.

Why Use Computers to Teach Writing?

- **Students are able to produce legible text.** Due to the many errors students make while writing, creating a neat and legible document with pencil or pen becomes an arduous task in itself. For some, this task alone can completely block the writing process. Certainly it is the major reason for students' resistance to editing documents.

- **By separating the planning and writing steps of the writing process, segmentation of the process becomes inherent in the program rather than a forced element.** Students resist breaking their writing into specific steps for many reasons. Using the computer with separate programs for planning and writing not only forces this segmenta-

---

> ## Why Use Computers?
>
> - ▶ Produce legible text
> - ▶ Direct the writing process (planning, writing, editing)
> - ▶ Increase fluent production of sentences
> - ▶ Encourage elaboration
> - ▶ Guide organization
> - ▶ Enhance student self-esteem

tion but also reinforces the difference between the two tasks.

- **Using the outline developed in the planning steps increases the fluent production of sentences.** Students write sentences using prompts that focus them on the ideas they are trying to communicate, one sentence at a time. This way the writing stage is broken into manageable parts.

- **Writing in a sentence-by-sentence fashion encourages more elaborate writing.** Dealing with one sentence at a time, students more readily expand their sentences thereby developing more complex writing. Students use skills already mastered in previous learning.

- **Matching outline and organizer, and using a consistent color code throughout the program forces organization.**

> ## The Term 'Web Templates'
>
> Web templates are not downloaded from the Internet. They are graphic templates that help students visually organize their thoughts prior to writing. They are provided on the CD-ROM that accompanies this text.

Web templates are used in the planning phase to organize information in the proper sequence for a particular paragraph type (The Structured Writing program introduces several types of paragraphs). Writing organizers matched to the outlines generated from the web allow the transfer of the structural sequence to the written document by arranging the sentences in the proper sequence. The color code allows students to visually check the draft document to ensure the structure has been followed throughout the process.

- **Rapid success creating documents that meet teacher expectations enhances students' self-esteem.** One of the most important factors in becoming a competent writer is the belief that one can succeed. Students who question their abilities to produce acceptable work develop patterns of resistance that can prevent the possibility of success. By eliminating failure in the early stages, students develop a view of themselves as competent writers. This view is one of the most important factors effecting later success as writers.

Why Use Templates to Teach Writing?

- **Templates define and teach the structure of essential paragraph elements.** Students who have difficulty learning from visual and oral direction often find success through the tactile path. Writing templates accurately guide these students through the task.

- **Color coding reinforces of the structural elements of the paragraph through visual recognition.** Constant repetition of the color code re-teaches the paragraph structure each time a student writes a paragraph. This re-

Why Use Templates?

- ▶ Templates define the structure of essential elements of the writing
- ▶ Color-coded for visual recognition
- ▶ Follows from the simple to the complex pattern
- ▶ Rapid improvement increases student motivation

teaching and practice is essential for mastery of the task.

- **The entire writing process flows from the simple to the complex.** Students are taught in direct managable steps. Introducing one or two new concepts at each step with direct instruction, the students can learn the task without becoming overwhelmed. Practicing each step until the students have mastered the concept allows each student to focus only on the new information at hand.

- **Students are encouraged and further motivated by their rapid improvement.** Nothing breeds success like success. Most students with writing difficulties have not experienced much success in their academic endeavors. This program guarantees success if the steps are followed. Students respond to this process and want more success. They are motivated to attempt more difficult writing tasks and to move forward through the entire writing process.

Technical Considerations

We use two computer programs as tools in the Structured Writing process. These programs were chosen for their ease of use

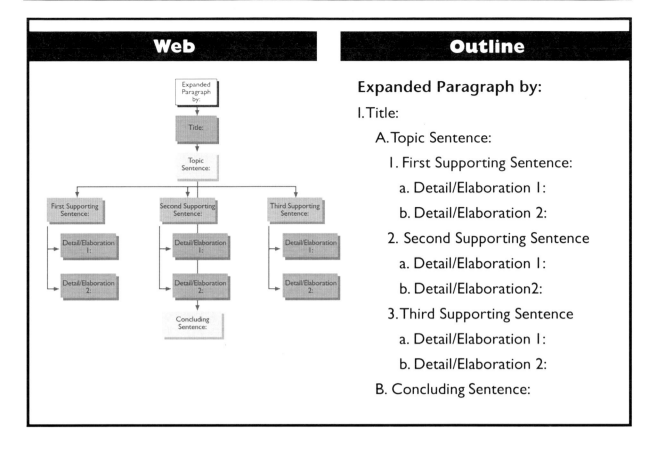

Web	Outline

(diagram: Expanded Paragraph by: → Title: → Topic Sentence: → First Supporting Sentence:, Second Supporting Sentence:, Third Supporting Sentence:, each with Detail/Elaboration 1: and Detail/Elaboration 2:, and Concluding Sentence:)	**Expanded Paragraph by:**
	I. Title:
	  A. Topic Sentence:
	    1. First Supporting Sentence:
	      a. Detail/Elaboration 1:
	      b. Detail/Elaboration 2:
	    2. Second Supporting Sentence
	      a. Detail/Elaboration 1:
	      b. Detail/Elaboration2:
	    3. Third Supporting Sentence
	      a. Detail/Elaboration 1:
	      b. Detail/Elaboration 2:
	  B. Concluding Sentence:

and identical cross platform formats when using either a Windows or Macintosh operating system. Inspiration is used for the planning step of the writing process. We create templates in a web form which are easily converted to an outline that guides the writing steps (see above).

Any word processor can be used for the writing step. We have chosen Write: OutLoud 3.0 because of its ease of use when moving between the Macintosh and Windows platforms and because of its effectiveness with special education students. It also has a speaking spell checker and dictionary built into both versions. The Structured Writing CD-ROM includes stationery organizers for Write:OutLoud 3.0, AppleWorks 5.0 and 6.0, Microsoft Word, and in a RTF (rich text format) that can be used in any other word processing program. We create **organizers** in the stationery format to use for the initial writing step. These organizers are matched in structure and color code with

the outlines prepared in Inspiration (see next page).

Students use the editing features of their word processing programs to edit their documents and use the text-to-speech features to proof read the document. Using these two software tools, students are able to transverse the entire writing process and create acceptable written documents independently.

As mentioned earlier, the teaching sequence is from the simple to the complex. Students must be able to write a coherent sentence before attempting a paragraph. Likewise, students must be able to write simple, basic paragraphs before attempting more complicated paragraphs of specific types. Structured Writing teaches writing skills in the following order:

♦ Basic five-sentence paragraphs

♦ Expanded paragraphs

Outline	Organizer
Expanded Paragraph Outline by:	Expanded Paragraph Organizer by:
I. Title:	Title:
A. Topic Sentence:	Topic Sentence:
1. First Supporting Sentence:	First Supporting Sentence:
a. Detail/Elaboration 1:	Detail/Elaboration 1:
b. Detail/Elaboration 2:	Detail/Elaboration 2:
2. Second Supporting Sentence	Second Supporting Sentence
a. Detail/Elaboration 1:	Detail/Elaboration 1:
b. Detail/Elaboration2:	Detail/Elaboration2:
3. Third Supporting Sentence	Third Supporting Sentence
a. Detail/Elaboration 1:	Detail/Elaboration 1:
b. Detail/Elaboration 2:	Detail/Elaboration 2:
B. Concluding Sentence:	Concluding Sentence:

- ◆ Reason paragraphs
- ◆ Example paragraphs
- ◆ Process paragraphs
- ◆ Classification paragraphs
- ◆ Compare and Contrast paragraphs

As we move through the sequence, you will notice the increasing complexity, and along with that, we also expect the variety and complexity of the sentences used to increase. Students should not move to a new paragraph type before they are comfortable with the previous paragraph type.

Optional Posters

In each lesson, the "Materials needed" section suggests the use of posters which teachers can hang up in their classrooms. To make these posters, the paragraph webs in the following chapters can be photocopied or printed from the accompanying CD-ROM. The Contents lists the pages where the posters can be found.

Chapter 1

Structured Writing—The Process

Structured Writing is a method to teach the process of paragraph writing using computer templates.

Many students state that they do not know what is expected of them when given a writing assignment. Structured Writing gives explicit instructions of the teacher's expectations. Experience has shown that explicit, step-by-step instructions increase the chances of success for these students.

Within the Structured Writing process, templates identify the required writing components of the assignment. Students can easily see the required format for each assignment by looking at a color-coded web/outline provided by the teacher in the planning step of the writing process. In this way, the teacher's expectations of the content to be covered in the writing assignment are clearly defined.

Structured Writing process:

- ◆ Planning
- ◆ Writing
- ◆ Editing/Revising
- ◆ Formatting
- ◆ Publishing

- **Planning step:** An Inspiration 6.0 web template is used to organize ideas and generate an **outline** to guide writing.

- **Writing step:** A word-processing **organizer** template (Write:OutLoud) is color coded to match the Inspiration outline and allows the student to expand and organize his or her ideas into a paragraph, one sentence at a time.

- **Editing/revising step:** Using the editing functions of a word-processing program, the student corrects capitalization, punctuation, and spelling errors. The student expands his or her sentences using modifiers, adjectives, adverbs, and prepositional phrases. Students vary sentence structure and enhance vocabulary by using the thesaurus.

- **Formatting step:** The words provided in the template are removed from the document leaving only the students' work. Sentences are placed into paragraph or draft form. Students reread to ensure they have used proper transition words in the supporting sentences.

- **Publishing step:** After submission to a proofreader, the document is corrected, the color code removed, and the writing published as a final copy.

Deciding the order in which information is presented in a paragraph is difficult for many students. Structured Writing templates define that order and allow students to write paragraphs, **one sentence at a time**. Placing words and ideas in the template automatically puts them in the required sequence for each paragraph. Color-coding provides visual recognition of the essential elements of individual paragraphs.

Compared to writing a sentence, writing a paragraph can be a daunting task for many students. Writing a paragraph is made more manageable when written sentence-by-sentence. Structured Writing's focus on writing a document one sentence at a time forces an emphasis on content and discourages students from being sidetracked during the writing process. The electronic editing capabilities of computers assist students to efficiently and independently produce quality written work. The teacher can observe the students during the various steps in the writing process, assess individual difficulties, and intervene with instruction immediately. Planning, writing, revising, editing, and publishing are emphasized as separate steps in the writing process. Using Structured Writing and computer, teachers can guide students through the difficult process of paragraph writing.

Structured Writing paragraph sequence:

- ◆ Basic Paragraphs
- ◆ Expanded Paragraphs
- ◆ Reason Paragraphs
- ◆ Example Paragraphs
- ◆ Process Paragraphs
- ◆ Classification Paragraphs
- ◆ Compare and Contrast Paragraphs

Structured Writing begins with writing a simple, concrete sentence and expands to writing complex, expanded paragraphs. Each new writing concept is added on to that which has been previously learned, one concept at a time. Basic, five-sentence paragraphs are taught before making them into expanded paragraphs with more detail and elaboration.

Expanded expository paragraphs are separated into five different types: reason, example, process, classification, and compare and contrast. Varying sentence structure and using transitions to separate the supporting sentences are introduced here, as well as thesaurus instruction to vary words and incorporate a more complex vocabulary. Multiple paragraph essays are introduced by having students take their expanded paragraphs and using supporting sentences as topic sentences for the supporting paragraphs of an essay.

We believe that combining effective writing instruction with word processing enhances students' writing. The computer is a useful tool to teach writing for several reasons. First, the computer allows students to produce neatly printed, accurately spelled, readable text of which they can be proud. Use of the computer spell checker significantly increases spelling accuracy, and producing a paper that looks professional

Structured Writing Tools

Inspiration 6.0
▶ Web (template)
▶ Outline

Write:Outloud 3.0
▶ Organizer (template)
▶ Editing/Revising

raises students' self-esteem. Secondly, the ease of making multiple edits eliminates the tedious and frustrating task of rewriting and revising by hand. Students are free to express themselves and to use words they aren't sure how to spell, knowing they will edit their writing at the next step. This freedom from tedious hand-written revisions also encourages students to elaborate more.

Using specific software for each step reinforces the sequential nature of the writing process. Inspiration, a web/outline program, is used for the planning step of the writing process. The web templates provided help organize and outline thoughts and ideas. Customized templates created for the various types of paragraphs (included on the **Structured Writing CD-ROM**) provide the specific structure for the various paragraphs. The essential elements of the paragraphs are color coded for visual recognition and to reinforce the parts of the paragraph. This visual display of the whole paragraph teaches the basic structure of each paragraph visually and reinforces that structure each time the student writes a paragraph.

A word-processing program (Write:OutLoud) is used to write and expand the single words and short phrases from the outline into complete sentences in the writing step. Although we have chosen

Write:OutLoud, other word processing programs that allow color text can be used. Customized organizer templates that coordinate with the outlines from Inspiration are used to guide writing and expand the single words and short phrases from the outlines into complete sentences. The color code of the organizer matches that of the outline to further reinforce the essential elements of the paragraph. Sentences are composed one at a time in the same sequence as the outline.

Finally, specific editing steps use both the spell checker and text-to-speech features of the word-processing program, allowing students to thoroughly and independently edit their work before giving it to a proofreader. Removal of the color code is the last editing step. The publishing step indicates completion of the process.

Using the computer and the Structured Writing process provides the organization that makes writing effective paragraphs achievable for most students. The color-coded outlines and organizers alert the students to the essential elements of paragraphs and communicate the teacher's expectations. Whether a student has a plethora of ideas to write about, or is stifled by writer's block, the Structured Writing system has a place for every thought and element required. It provokes and cues ideas for students who have difficulty knowing what to write.

Each step of the writing process is part of the structured lessons, yet the computer eliminates the fear many students have of recopying. Teachers can observe the students' writing at the various steps, assess difficulties, and intervene with instruction immediately. Students' self-esteem regarding their writing is enhanced using Structured Writing because they end up with logically sequenced, accurately spelled, quality documents that meet the teacher's expectations.

Paragraph Writing Requirements

#1 Outline:

    Inspiration template
    Use single words and short phrases
    Topic and concluding sentences must be complete
    SAVE AS "title, outline"
    Print in color

#2 Organizer:

    An organizer stationery
    Expand words to complete sentences
    Transition for each green structure sentence
    Edit and spell check
    Vary sentence structure
    Use thesaurus
    SAVE AS "title, organizer #__"
    Print in color

#3 Draft:

    Format
    Name and date
    Remove structure headings
    Adjust spacing between sentences and after ending punctuation
    SAVE AS "title, draft #__"
    Print in color
    Give to proof reader for final edit

#4 Final copy:

    Change to black
    SAVE AS "title, final copy"
    Print

Editing Steps

- ▶ **Save after writing**
- ▶ **Read/listen to sentences**
  - • **Content**
  - • **Capitalization**
  - • **Punctuation**
  - • **Word usage**
- ▶ **Spell check**
- ▶ **Save corrected copy**
- ▶ **Reread/listen**
  - • **Word usage**
  - • **Content**
- ▶ **Save corrected draft**
  - • **Format draft (title, indent, spacing)**
- ▶ **Have a proof reader edit**
- ▶ **Save corrected copy**
- ▶ **Print final copy**

Chapter 2

The Basic Paragraph Lesson

Objectives:

1. Students will write a five-sentence Basic Paragraph using a title, a topic sentence, three supporting sentences, and a concluding sentence.

2. Students will learn the color codes, reinforcing the essential elements of the paragraph: blue for title, yellow for topic and concluding sentences, green for supporting sentences.

3. Students will use the steps of the Structured Writing process to plan, write, edit, and publish a basic, five-sentence paragraph.

4. Students will use the sequential Structured Writing editing steps to read and listen, to check the writing content, capitalization and punctuation, and to run the spell checker.

Materials needed:

1. Structured Writing CD-ROM

   a. Structured Writing Basic Paragraph Web

   b. Structured Writing Basic Paragraph Organizer

2. Inspiration 6.0

3. Word-processing program (Write:Outloud)

4. Paragraph Writing Requirements poster (optional)

5. Editing Steps poster (optional)

Essential elements:

The Structured Writing Process teaches students to write a Basic Paragraph using:

1. A topic sentence

2. Three supporting sentences

3. A concluding sentence

Color codes:

♦ Blue for title

♦ Yellow for topic and concluding sentences

♦ Green for supporting sentences

The writing process:

1. Planning step (Outline)

2. Writing step (Organizer)

3. Editing step (Edited organizer)

4. Formatting step (Draft)

5. Publishing step (Final copy)

The editing process:

1. Save in the appropriate folder or directory.

2. Use text-to-speech to read and listen to each sentence, one at a time.

3. Check capitalization and punctuation.

4. Use a thesaurus and vary sentence structure.

5. Read and listen.

6. Run spell checker.

7. Print in color and give to a proofreader to edit.

The Structured Writing Basic Paragraph Process

The Planning Step

Students begin the planning step by opening the Inspiration template titled *Basic Paragraph Web*, available on the accompanying CD-ROM. This template helps them organize their thoughts for writing. The color code and the text help identify the essential elements of the paragraph: title, topic, three supporting ideas, and a conclusion.

Model the lesson by assigning the topic "**My Pets.**"

1. The white box in the web indicates a place for the student's name, the blue box is for the paragraph title, and the yellow boxes are for the topic and concluding ideas. The three green boxes below the topic sentence signify the place for supporting thoughts and ideas.

2. Students keyboard only single words and short phrases into the web to represent these ideas. **Reinforce the concept of outlining as idea organization, not sentence writing.** The words and phrases will later be converted into an outline. The outline will be used as a guide to creating full sentences during the writing step using the Structured Writing organizer template. This step may seem unnecessary for a simple paragraph, but it is essential for training students to outline as a fundamental part of the writing process.

3. Students convert the web into a color-coded outline by selecting the outline option in Inspiration and running spell check to make initial corrections. Inspiration's spell checker can be difficult for some students to use. If this problem arises, defer spell checking to the first editing step. Students save their outlines in the appropriate file or directory.

4. Students print the color-coded outline and give it to the teacher who checks the content and gives the students feedback. Reassured that the content is appropriate, students use this outline to continue with the next step of the writing process, the writing step.

Basic Paragraph Web

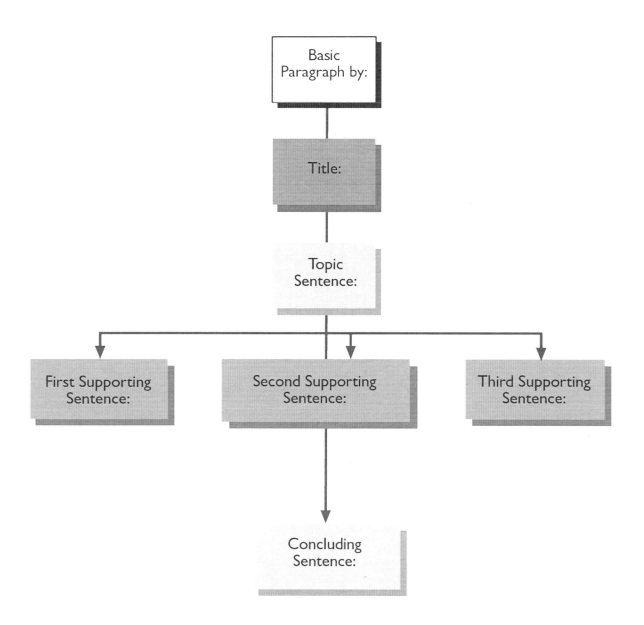

Basic Paragraph by:

Title:

Topic Sentence:

First Supporting Sentence:

Second Supporting Sentence:

Third Supporting Sentence:

Concluding Sentence:

Basic Paragraph Example

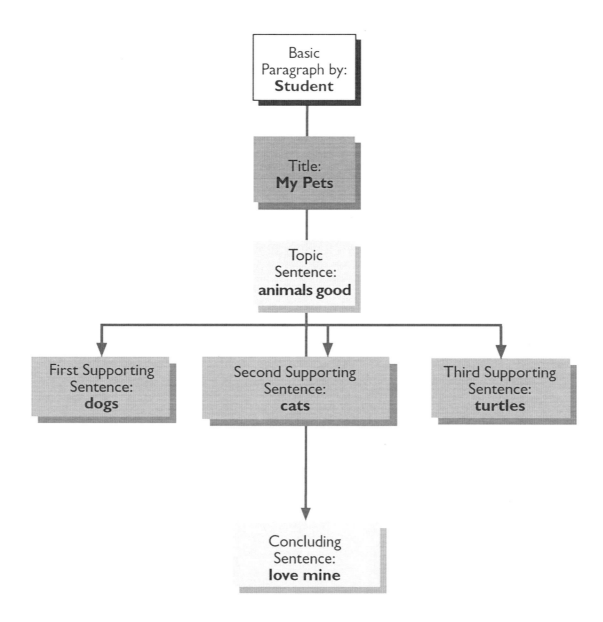

The Writing Step

Students use the color-coded Structured Writing *Basic Paragraph Organizer* and a word-processing program (Write:Outloud) to guide and expand their one-word ideas from the outline into complete sentences.

1. Using the outline as a guide, students create complete sentences in the organizer, one at a time. Each sentence will be revised later and edited during the editing step, one sentence at a time.

2. Students expand and elaborate their sentences as they write.

3. Once all the sentences are completed, students save the organizer in the proper folder or directory.

4. At this point, the teacher assesses the document for sentence structure and suggests expanding terms when appropriate.

The Editing Step

Students are required to use a specific editing process to make sure they wrote what they meant to convey and to correct spelling and mechanical errors. This step becomes more complex as the students proceed through the Structured Writing sequence.

1. Students use text-to-speech to read and listen to each sentence, **one at a time**. Here, students add, delete and change words until the sentences sound right and communicate what they mean.

2. Students check capitalization (the beginning of each sentence and proper nouns) and punctuation, word usage, and spelling. We recommend that students be taught to do this editing in the specific order. Using the spell checker in the word processor as the last step gives students a better chance to properly correct misspelled words.

Basic Paragraph Outline by:

I. Title:
  A. Topic Sentence:
    1. First Supporting Sentence:
    2. Second Supporting Sentence:
    3. Third Supporting Sentence:
  B. Concluding Sentence:

Basic Paragraph Organizer by:

Title:
Topic Sentence:
First Supporting Sentence:
Second Supporting Sentence:
Third Supporting Sentence:
Concluding Sentence:

Basic Paragraph Outline by: Student

I. Title: My Pets
  A. Topic Sentence: animals good
    1. First Supporting Sentence: dogs
    2. Second Supporting Sentence: cats
    3. Third Supporting Sentence: turtles
  B. Concluding Sentence: love mine

Basic Paragraph Organizer by: Student

Title: My Pets
Topic Sentence: I have four pets.
First Supporting Sentence: My dog is named Sandy.
Second Supporting Sentence: I have two cats named Bert and Ernie.
Third Supporting Sentence: My box turtle lives in a heated aquarium in my room.
Concluding Sentence: I love my pets.

3. Students make sure that the three supporting sentences support the topic sentence, then save the edited organizer in the appropriate folder or directory.

4. The teacher evaluates the sentences again for structure and proper syntax and give feedback to the students. Secure that the syntax, grammar, structure and spelling are correct, students move to the formatting step.

Student
Date

My Pets

I have four pets. My dog is named Sandy. I have two cats named Bert and Ernie. My box turtle lives in a heated aquarium in my room. I love my pets.

The Formatting Step

In this step, students remove the words provided in the template from the organizer, leaving only the students' work. The students put the sentences into paragraph form as a draft.

1. Students highlight the structure words and colons and delete them. As each structure word is deleted, students sequence the sentences one after the other, paying attention to beginning capitalization, ending punctuation, and spacing between sentences and lines.

2. Under "name," students add the day's date and any other information that belongs in the heading.

3. Students center the title and check words for proper capitalization.

4. Students indent the topic sentence.

5. Students read and listen again to the paragraph as a whole, assessing the flow and continuity of their ideas.

6. Students save the document as '*draft*' in the proper folder or directory and print it out in color, providing a copy to a proofreader to edit.

The Publishing Step

At this point, when students receive approved drafts, the writing process is completed except for removing the color and printing a final copy.

1. Students change the text color to black.

2. Students save the file in the appropriate folder or directory as '*final copy*' and print a final copy in black.

3. Students submit a completed packet containing the outline, organizer, draft, and final copy.

This may sound like a tedious, overwhelming task as you read all the steps at once for writing one little paragraph. However, our experience with students having difficulty writing is that this structure and sequence makes it possible for them to write coherent paragraphs.

In summary, the Basic Paragraph is used to teach the student how to use the structured writing process to write a paragraph. The concepts taught using the Basic Paragraph are:

♦ Three essential elements of a paragraph
  • Topic sentence
  • Three support sentences
  • Concluding sentence

- ◆ Color code for each of the Basic Paragraph parts
- ◆ Four steps of the writing process and the paragraph writing requirements for each step
- ◆ The steps of the editing process

The writing process is the same throughout this program. Students follow the same process for each type of paragraph. The planning and outlining steps use Inspiration and teacher-created templates. The writing step uses a word-processing program and teacher-created templates. The revising and editing steps follow the same sequence for all paragraphs. The Structured Writing process culminates with the formatting and publishing steps. Though the paragraph types vary, the Structured Writing process and sequence remain the same.

After students write many Basic Paragraphs on various topics, teachers should assess the students' mastery of the writing process steps. Once the process is mastered, it is time to move on to more complex paragraphs. The next step up in complexity is the Expanded Paragraph. The writing steps remain consistent throughout instruction.

Suggested Topics for Basic Paragraphs

- Snacks
- Games
- Hobbies
- Things to do at recess
- Families

- Books
- Movies
- Desserts
- Holidays

Chapter 3

The Expanded Paragraph Lesson

Objectives:

1. Students will write an Expanded Paragraph using a title, a topic sentence, three supporting sentences with **transition words, two detail sentences elaborating each supporting sentence**, and a concluding sentence.

2. Students will learn the color codes, reinforcing the essential elements of the paragraph: blue for title, yellow for topic and concluding sentences, green for supporting sentences, and **pink for details.**

3. Students will use the steps of the Structured Writing process to plan, write, edit, and publish an Expanded Paragraph.

4. Students will use the sequential editing steps in Structured Writing. They will use text-to-speech features to read and listen while checking the writing content, capitalization and punctuation, and running the spell checker.

Materials needed:

1. Structured Writing CD-ROM

   a. Structured Writing Expanded Paragraph Web

   b. Structured Writing Expanded Paragraph Organizer

2. Inspiration 6.0

3. Word-processing program (Write:Outloud)

4. Paragraph Requirements poster (optional)

5. Editing Steps poster (optional)

6. Transition Words poster (optional)

Essential elements:

The Structured Writing process teaches students to write an Expanded Paragraph using:

1. A topic sentence

2. Three supporting sentences with **transition words**

3. **Two detail sentences** for each supporting sentence

4. A concluding sentence

Color codes:

- ◆ Blue for title
- ◆ Yellow for topic and concluding sentences
- ◆ Green for supporting sentences
- ◆ **Pink** for detail sentences

The writing process:

1. Planning step (Outline)
2. Writing step (Organizer)
3. Editing step (Edited organizer)
4. Formatting step (Draft)
5. Publishing step (Final copy)

The editing process:

1. Save in the appropriate folder or directory.
2. Use text-to-speech to read and listen to each sentence, one at a time.
3. Check capitalization and punctuation.
4. Use **transition words and a thesaurus, and vary sentence structure.**
5. Read and listen.
6. Run spell checker.
7. Print in color and give to a proofreader to edit.

The Structured Writing Expanded Paragraph Process

The Planning Step

Students begin the planning step by opening the Inspiration template titled *Expanded Paragraph Web*, available on the accompanying CD-ROM. This template helps them organize their thoughts for writing. The color code and the text help identify the essential elements of the paragraph: title, topic, three supporting ideas, **two details for each supporting idea**, and a conclusion.

Model the lesson by assigning the topic **"My Pets."**

1. The white box in the web indicates a place for the student's name, the blue box is for the paragraph title, and the yellow boxes are for the topic and concluding ideas. The three green boxes below the topic sentence signify the place for supporting thoughts and ideas. **The two pink boxes will hold the details for each supporting idea**.

2. Students keyboard only single words and short phrases in the web to represent these ideas. **Reinforce the concept of outlining as idea organization, not sentence writing.** The words and phrases will be converted into an outline to use as a guide for writing sentences in the organizer during the writing step of this process. This step may seem unnecessary for a simple paragraph, but it is essential for training students to outline as a fundamental part of the writing process.

3. Students convert the web into a color-coded outline by selecting the outline option in Inspiration and running spell check to make initial corrections. Inspiration's spell checker can be difficult for some students to use. If this problem arises, defer spell checking to the first editing step. Students save their outlines in the appropriate folder or directory.

Expanded Paragraph Web

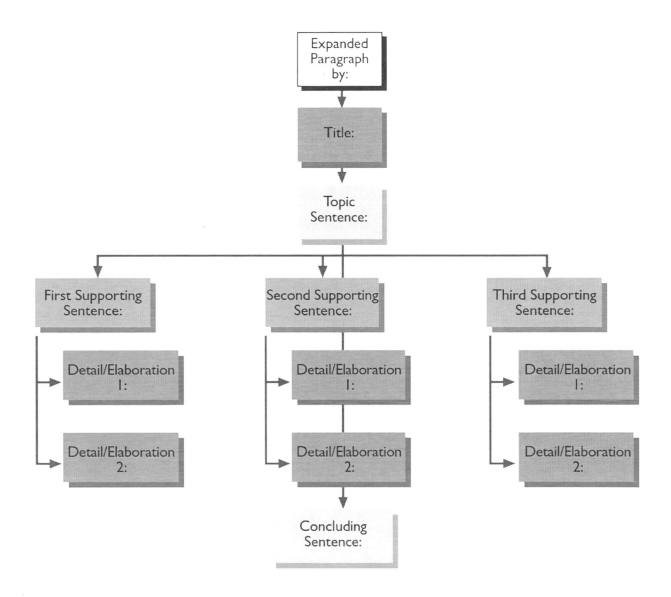

Expanded
Paragraph
by:

Title:

Topic
Sentence:

First Supporting
Sentence:

Second Supporting
Sentence:

Third Supporting
Sentence:

Detail/Elaboration
1:

Detail/Elaboration
1:

Detail/Elaboration
1:

Detail/Elaboration
2:

Detail/Elaboration
2:

Detail/Elaboration
2:

Concluding
Sentence:

Expanded Paragraph Example

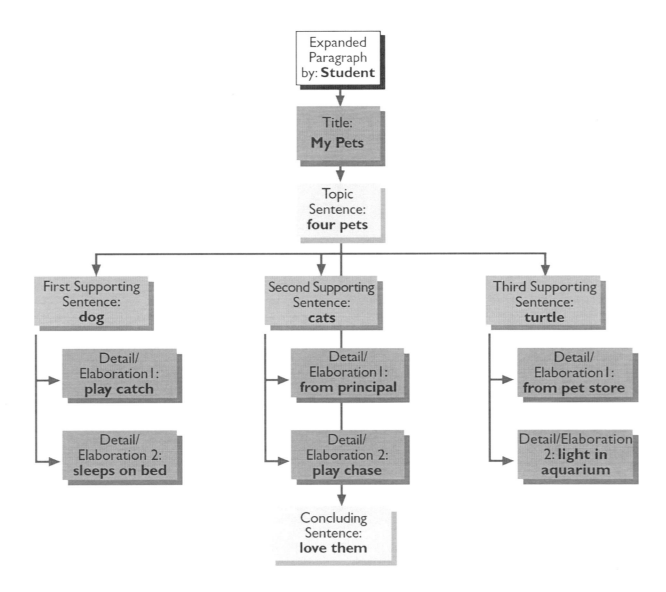

Expanded Paragraph Outline by:	Expanded Paragraph Organizer by:

I. Title:
   A. Topic Sentence:
      1. First Supporting Sentence:
         a. Detail/Elaboration 1:
         b. Detail/Elaboration 2:
      2. Second Supporting Sentence:
         a. Detail/Elaboration 1:
         b. Detail/Elaboration 2:
      3. Third Supporting Sentence:
         a. Detail/Elaboration 1:
         b. Detail/Elaboration 2:
   B. Concluding Sentence:
	Title:
	Topic Sentence:
	First Supporting Sentence:
	Detail/Elaboration 1:
	Detail/Elaboration 2:
	Second Supporting Sentence:
	Detail/Elaboration 1:
	Detail/Elaboration 2:
	Third Supporting Sentence:
	Detail/Elaboration 1:
	Detail/Elaboration 2:
	Concluding Sentence:

4. Students print the color-coded outline and give it to the teacher, who checks the content and gives the students feedback. Reassured that the content is appropriate, students use this outline to continue with the next step of the writing process, the writing step.

The Writing Step

Students use the color-coded Structured Writing *Expanded Paragraph Organizer* and a word-processing program (Write:Outloud) as a guide to expand their ideas from the outline into complete sentences in the organizer, one at a time.

1. Using the outline as a guide, students create complete sentences in the organizer, one at a time. Each sentence will be revised later and edited in the editing step, one sentence at a time.

2. Students expand and elaborate their sentences as they write. Teachers direct students to **use adjectives, adverbs, and prepositional phrases** to expand and clarify their writing, and to combine simple sentences into compound sentences.

3. Teachers should focus on **two new concepts** while teaching the Expanded Paragraph. To make the detailed explanation clear, students add **supporting sentences which are identified by transition words** to point the reader toward main supporting statements. **Each supporting sentence needs two detail sentences to expand the explanation.** Teachers alert students to the different transition words they can use. Posting these examples helps students use transition words with confidence.

4. Once all the sentences are completed, the students save the organizer in the proper folder or directory.

5. At this point, the teacher assesses the document for sentence structure and suggests expanding terms when appropriate.

The Editing Step

Students are required to use a specific editing process to make sure their sentences reflect what they meant to convey and to correct spelling and mechanical errors. This step becomes more complex as the students

---

Expanded Paragraph Outline by: Student

I. Title: My Pets
    A. Topic Sentence: four pets
        1. First Supporting Sentence: dog
            a. Detail/Elaboration 1: play catch
            b. Detail/Elaboration 2: sleeps on bed
        2. Second Supporting Sentence: cats
            a. Detail/Elaboration 1: from principal
            b. Detail/Elaboration 2: play chase
        3. Third Supporting Sentence: turtle
            a. Detail/Elaboration 1: from pet store
            b. Detail/Elaboration 2: light in aquarium
    B. Concluding Sentence: love them

---

proceed through the Structured Writing sequence.

1. Students use text-to-speech to read and listen to each sentence, **one at a time**. Here, students add, delete, and change words until the sentences sound right and communicate what they mean.

2. Students check capitalization (the beginning of each sentence and proper nouns) and punctuation, word usage, and spelling. We recommend that students be taught to do this editing in the specific order. Using the spell checker in the word processor as the last step gives students a better chance to properly correct misspelled words.

3. Students make sure to include appropriate **transition words** at the beginning of each supporting sentence. Students check to ensure details elaborate each supporting sentence.

4. During editing, after the initial structure, sequence, and purpose has been set, **students then revise sentences to refine the paragraph**. These skills are taught only when the students are

---

Expanded Paragraph Organizer by: Student

Title: My Pets
Topic Sentence: I have four pets.
First Supporting Sentence: First of all, Sandy is my Golden Retriever.
Detail/Elaboration 1: She likes to play catch with a tennis ball.
Detail/Elaboration 2: She sleeps on my bed at night.
Second Supporting Sentence: Secondly, I have two cats named Bert and Ernie.
Detail/Elaboration 1: The principal at my school gave them to me.
Detail/Elaboration 2: They like to play chase with each other.
Third Supporting Sentence: Finally, Slow Poke is my box turtle.
Detail/Elaboration 1: Dad bought him for me at the pet store.
Detail/Elaboration 2: He has a light in his aquarium to keep him warm.
Concluding Sentence: Sandy, Bert and Ernie, and Slow Poke are the best pets in the world.

---

secure in their ability to clearly write an expanded paragraph. Students need to **vary the structure of their sentences** (imperative, declarative, interrogatory, exclamatory), and **use the thesaurus** to develop a more complex vocabulary. **This expansion is not meant to increase creativity but to produce a more specific explanation of a concept.**

5. Students save the edited organizer in the proper folder or directory.

6. Teachers assess the sentences for structure, variation, the use of transition words, and proper syntax to give feedback to the students. Reassured that syntax, grammar, structure and spelling are correct, students move to the formatting step.

The Formatting Step

In this step, students remove the structure words from the organizer and put the sentences into paragraph form as a draft.

1. Students highlight the structure words and colons and delete them. As each structure word is deleted, students sequence the sentences one after the other, paying attention to beginning capitalization, ending punctuation, and spacing between sentences and lines.

2. Under "name," students add the day's date and any other information that belongs in the heading.

3. Students center the title and check for proper capitalization.

4. Students indent the topic sentence.

5. Students read and listen again to the paragraph as a whole, assessing the flow and continuity of their ideas.

6. Students save the document as 'draft' in the proper folder or directory and print it out in color, providing a copy to a proofreader to edit.

The Publishing Step

At this point, when students receive approved drafts, the writing process is completed except for removing the color and printing a final copy.

1. Students change the text color to black.

2. Students save the file in the proper folder or directory as 'final copy' and print a final copy in black.

3. Students submit a completed packet containing the outline, organizer, draft, and final copy.

In summary, the Expanded Paragraph adds several new concepts to paragraph writing:

♦ Details to the supporting sentences

♦ Transition words for supporting statements

♦ Sentences expanded by adjectives, adverbs, and prepositional phrases

♦ Varied sentence structure

♦ Use of the thesaurus to enhance vocabulary

Students must practice and master each new paragraph type before moving on to a more complex one. Teachers must be sure that students follow all the writing steps correctly. Visual reminders (posters) displayed throughout the classroom and kept in student binders make a good reference.

After students practice writing specific Expanded Paragraphs on various topics, they can begin to write each of the five following types of expository paragraphs: **Reason, Example, Process, Classification,** and **Compare and Contrast**. The paragraph types are differentiated by the structure of the paragraph and the form of the supporting statements.

My Pets

Student
Date

I have four pets. First of all, Sandy is my Golden Retrieve. She likes to play catch with a tennis ball. She sleeps on my bed at night. Secondly, I have two cats named Bert and Ernie. The principal at my school gave them to me. They like to play chase with each other. Finally, Slow Poke is my box turtle. Dad bought him for me at the pet store. He has a light in his aquarium to keep him warm. Sandy, Bert and Ernie, and Slow Poke are the best pets in the world.

ordered, sequential steps in a process as supporting sentences, and a Classification Paragraph uses groupings or categories as supporting sentences. The Compare and Contrast Paragraph uses corresponding points of comparison between two items as supporting sentences.

The writing process is the same throughout this program. Students follow the same process for each type of paragraph. The planning and outlining steps use Inspiration and teacher-created templates. The writing step uses a word-processing program (Write:OutLoud) and teacher-created organizers. The revising and editing steps follow the same sequence for all writing. The Structured Writing process culminates with the formatting and publishing steps. Though the paragraph types vary, the Structured Writing process and sequence remain the same.

For instance, the Reason Paragraph uses reasons as supporting sentences. An Example Paragraph uses examples for supporting sentences. A Process Paragraph uses

Suggested Topics for Expanded Paragraphs

- Popular games
- Good friends
- Fast food
- Playing sports
- TV programs
- Hobbies
- Modes of transportation
- Camping

Chapter 4

The Reason Paragraph Lesson

Objectives:

1. Students will write a Reason Paragraph using a title, a topic sentence, **three supporting sentences using reasons** with transition words, **two detail sentences elaborating each reason**, and a concluding sentence.

2. Students will learn the color codes, reinforcing the essential elements of the paragraph: blue for title, yellow for topic and concluding sentences, green for supporting reasons, pink for details.

3. Students will use the steps of the Structured Writing process to plan, write, edit, and publish a Reason Paragraph.

4. Students will use the sequential editing steps in Structured Writing. They will use text-to-speech features to read and listen while checking the writing content, capitalization and punctuation, and to run the spell checker.

Materials needed:

1. Structured Writing CD-ROM

    a. Structured Writing Reason Paragraph Web

    b. Structured Writing Reason Paragraph Organizer

2. Inspiration 6.0

3. Word-processing program (Write:Outloud)

4. Paragraph Requirements poster (optional)

5. Editing Steps poster (optional)

6. Reason Paragraph Transition Words poster (optional)

Essential elements:

The Structured Writing process teaches students to write a Reason Paragraph using:

1. A topic sentence

2. Three supporting sentences **using reasons**

3. Two detail sentences supporting **each reason**

4. **Transition words for each supporting reason**

5. A concluding sentence

Color codes:

- ♦ Blue for title
- ♦ Yellow for topic and concluding sentences
- ♦ Green for supporting reasons
- ♦ Pink for details elaborating each reason

The writing process:

1. Planning step (Outline)
2. Writing step (Organizer)
3. Editing step (Edited organizer)
4. Formatting step (Draft)
5. Publishing step (Final copy)

The editing process:

1. Save in the appropriate folder or directory.
2. Use text-to-speech to read and listen to each sentence, one at a time.
3. Check capitalization and punctuation.
4. Use transition words and a thesaurus, and vary sentence structure.
5. Read and listen.
6. Run spell checker.
7. Print in color and give to a proofreader to edit.

The Structured Writing Reason Paragraph Process

The Planning Step

Students begin the planning step by opening the Inspiration template titled *Reason Paragraph Web*, available on the accompanying CD-ROM. This template helps them organize their thoughts for writing. The color code and the text help identify the essential elements of the paragraph: title, topic, three supporting reasons, two details for each supporting reason, and a conclusion.

Model the lesson by assigning a reason paragraph on the topic **"Why I Like Vacations."**

1. The white box in the web indicates a place for the student's name, the blue box is for the paragraph title, and the yellow boxes are for the topic and concluding ideas. The three green boxes below the topic signify the place for **supporting reasons**. The two pink boxes will hold the details for each supporting reason.

2. Students keyboard only single words and short phrases in the web to represent these ideas. **Reinforce the concept of outlining as idea organization, not sentence writing**. The words and phrases will be converted into an outline to use as a guide for writing sentences during the writing step of this process.

3. Students convert the web into a color-coded outline by selecting the outline option in Inspiration and running spell check to make initial spelling corrections. Inspiration's spell checker can be difficult for some students to use. If this problem arises, defer spell checking to the first editing step. Students save their outlines in the appropriate folder or directory.

4. Students print the color-coded outline and give it to the teacher, who checks the content and gives the students feedback. Reassured that the content is appropriate, students use this outline to

Reason Paragraph Web

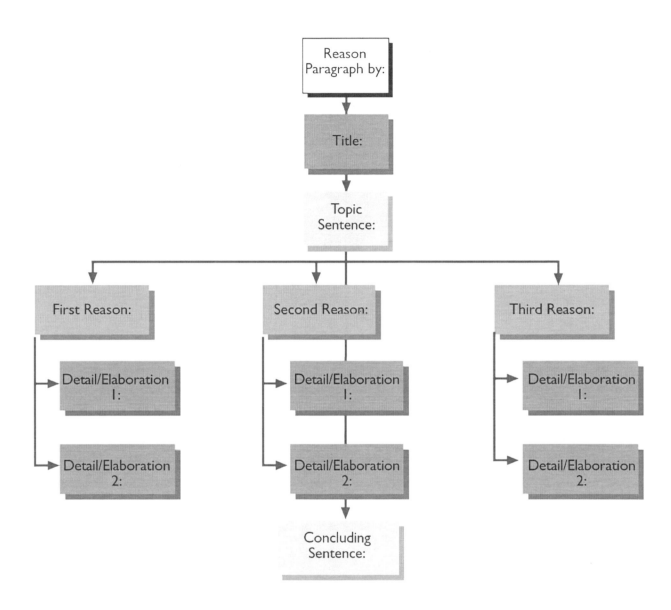

Reason Paragraph Example

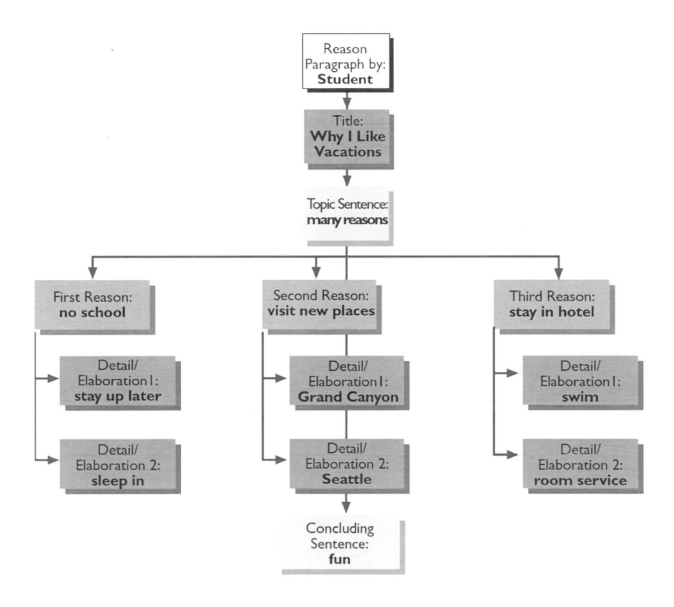

continue with the next step of the writing process, the writing step.

The Writing Step

Students use the color-coded Structured Writing *Reason Paragraph Organizer* and a word-processing program (Write:OutLoud) as a guide to expand their ideas from the outline into complete sentences, one at a time.

1. Using the outline as a guide, students create complete sentences in the organizer, one at a time. Each sentence will be revised later and edited in the editing step, sentence by sentence.

2. Students expand and elaborate their sentences as they write. They compose sentences using **reasons** that support their topic sentences. Teachers direct students to **use adjectives, adverbs, and prepositional phrases** to expand and clarify their writing, and to combine simple sentences into compound sentences.

3. Teachers focus on a single new concept while teaching students to write the Reason Paragraph: **Reasons are the supporting sentences**. To make the detailed explanation clear, students identify these supporting reasons by adding **transition words** that point the reader toward them. Teachers alert students to the reason transition words they can use. Posting these examples helps students use transition words with confidence.

4. Once all the sentences are completed, the students save the organizer in the proper folder or directory.

5. At this point, the teacher assesses the document for sentence structure and suggests expanding terms when appropriate.

The Editing Step

Students are required to use a specific editing process to make sure their sentences reflect what they mean to convey and to correct spelling and mechanical errors. This step becomes more complex as the students proceed through the Structured Writing sequence.

1. Students use text-to-speech to read and listen to each sentence, **one at a time**. Here, students add, delete, and change words until the sentences sound right and communicate what they mean.

Reason Paragraph Outline by:	Reason Paragraph Organizer by:
I. Title:	**Title:**
A. Topic Sentence:	**Topic Sentence:**
1. First Reason:	**First Reason:**
a. Detail/Elaboration 1:	**Detail/Elaboration 1:**
b. Detail/Elaboration 2:	**Detail/Elaboration 2:**
2. Second Reason:	**Second Reason:**
a. Detail/Elaboration 1:	**Detail/Elaboration 1:**
b. Detail/Elaboration 2:	**Detail/Elaboration 2:**
3. Third Reason:	**Third Reason:**
a. Detail/Elaboration 1:	**Detail/Elaboration 1:**
b. Detail/Elaboration 2:	**Detail/Elaboration 2:**
B. Concluding Sentence:	**Concluding Sentence:**

Reason Paragraph Outline by: Student

I. Title: Why I Like Vacations
    A. Topic Sentence: many reasons
        1. First Reason: no school
            a. Detail/Elaboration 1: stay up later
            b. Detail/Elaboration 2: sleep in
        2. Second Reason: visit new places
            a. Detail/Elaboration 1: see Grand Canyon
            b. Detail/Elaboration 2: Seattle
        3. Third Reason: stay in hotel
            a. Detail/Elaboration 1: swim
            b. Detail/Elaboration 2: room service
    B. Concluding Sentence: fun

2. Students check capitalization (the beginning of each sentence and proper nouns) and punctuation, word usage, and spelling. We recommend that students be taught to do this editing in the specific order. Using the spell checker in the word processor as the last step gives students a better chance to properly correct misspelled words.

3. Students make sure that three **reasons** support the topic sentence, and that appropriate **transition words** indicate each supporting sentence or reason.

4. During editing, after the initial structure, sequence, and purpose has been set, students then revise sentences to refine the paragraph. These skills are taught only when the students are secure in their ability to clearly write a reason paragraph. Students need to **vary the structure of their sentences** (imperative, declarative, interrogatory, exclamatory), and **use the thesaurus** to develop a more complex vocabulary. **This expansion is not meant to increase creativity but to produce a more specific explanation of a concept.**

5. Students save the edited organizer in the appropriate folder or directory.

6. Teachers assess the sentences for structure, variation, the use of transition words, and proper syntax to give feedback to the students. Reassured that syntax, grammar, structure, and spelling are correct, students move to the formatting step.

Reason Paragraph

Transition Words

- ▶ Each supporting idea is a new reason
- ▶ Use **transitions** to separate supporting reasons

- One reason, another reason, the last reason
- The first reason, the second reason, the third reason
- First of all, second, finally
- The first instance, the second instance, the third instance
- For instance
- Yet another reason
- The final reason

> **Reason Paragraph Organizer by:** Student
>
> **Title:** Why I Like Vacations
> **Topic Sentence:** There are many reasons why I like to go on vacation.
> **First Reason:** First of all, I like to go on vacation because I don't have to go to school.
> **Detail/Elaboration 1:** I can stay up later at night because I don't have to wake up early for school.
> **Detail/Elaboration 2:** I can sleep in later in the morning because I don't have to get up and go to school.
> **Second Reason:** A second reason I like to take vacations is because I like to visit new places.
> **Detail/Elaboration 1:** I want to see the Grand Canyon.
> **Detail/Elaboration 2:** I want to go and see my cousin in Seattle and ride the ferry boats.
> **Third Reason:** The third reason I like to go on vacation is because I like to stay in hotels.
> **Detail/Elaboration 1:** I like to swim in hotel swimming pools.
> **Detail/Elaboration 2:** I really like to order room service, especially for breakfast.
> **Concluding Sentence:** These are just three reasons why I like to go on vacation.

The Formatting Step

In this step, students remove the structure words from the organizer and put the sentences into paragraph form as a draft.

1. Students highlight the structure words and colons and delete them. As each structure word is deleted, students sequence the sentences one after the other paying attention to beginning capitalization, ending punctuation, and spacing between sentences and lines.

2. Under "name," students add the day's date and any other information that belongs in the heading.

3. Students center the title and check words for proper capitalization.

4. Students indent the topic sentence.

5. Students read and listen again to the paragraph as a whole, assessing the flow and continuity of their ideas.

6. Students save the document as *'draft'* in the proper folder or directory and print it out in color, providing a copy to a proofreader to edit.

The Publishing Step

At this point, when students receive approved drafts, the writing process is completed except for removing the color and printing a final copy.

1. Students change the text color to black removing the color.

2. Students save the file in the appropriate folder or directory as *'final copy'* and print in black.

3. Students submit a completed packet containing the outline, organizer, draft, and final copy.

Student
Date

Why I Like Vacations

There are many reasons why I like to go on vacation. First of all, I like to go on vacation because I don't have to go to school. I can stay up later at night because I don't have to wake up early for school. I can sleep in later in the morning because I don't have to get up and go to school. A second reason I like to take vacations is because I like to visit new places. I want to see the Grand Canyon. I want to go and see my cousin in Seattle and ride the ferryboats. The third reason I like to go on vacation is because I like to stay in hotels. I like to swim in hotel swimming pools. I really like to order room service, especially for breakfast. These are just three reasons why I like to go on vacation.

In summary, the Reason Paragraph modifies the Expanded Paragraph by using:

◆ **Reasons** as supporting sentences

◆ **Reason** transition words

Students must practice and master each new paragraph type before moving on to a more complex one. Teachers must be sure that students follow all the writing steps correctly. Visual reminders (posters) displayed throughout the classroom and kept in student binders make a good reference.

The writing process is the same throughout this program. Students follow the same process for each type of paragraph. The planning and outlining steps use Inspiration and teacher-created templates. The writing step uses a word-processing program (Write:OutLoud) and teacher-created organizers. The revising and editing steps follow the same sequence for all writing. The Structured Writing process culminates with the formatting and publishing steps. Though the paragraph types vary, the Structured Writing process and sequence remain the same.

Suggested Topics for Reason Paragraphs

- Why I like_____ (Christmas, Halloween, Thanksgiving, etc.)
- Why I use a computer
- Why water conservation is important
- Don't play with matches

- Why I play _____ (lacrosse, basketball, football, baseball, soccer, etc.)
- Advantages of doing well in school
- Why camping is fun
- A good book

Chapter 5

The Example Paragraph Lesson

Objectives:

1. Students will write an Example Paragraph using a title, a topic sentence, **three supporting sentences using examples** with transition words, **three detail sentences elaborating each example**, and a concluding sentence.

2. Students will learn the color codes, reinforcing the essential elements of the paragraph: blue for title, yellow for topic and concluding sentences, green for supporting examples, and pink for details.

3. Students will use the steps of the Structured Writing process to plan, write, edit, and publish an Example Paragraph.

4. Students will use the sequential editing steps in Structured Writing. They will use text-to-speech features to read and listen while checking the writing content, capitalization and punctuation, and running the spell checker.

Materials needed:

1. Structured Writing CD-ROM
   a. Structured Writing Example Paragraph Web

   b. Structured Writing Example Paragraph Organizer

2. Inspiration 6.0

3. Word-processing program (Write:Outloud)

4. Paragraph Requirements poster (optional)

5. Editing Steps poster (optional)

6. Example Transition Words poster (optional)

Essential elements:

The Structured Writing process teaches students to write an Example Paragraph using:

1. A topic sentence

2. Three supporting sentences **using examples**

3. **Three detail sentences** supporting **each example**

4. **Transition words for each supporting example**

5. A concluding sentence

Color codes:

- ◆ Blue for title
- ◆ Yellow for topic and concluding sentences
- ◆ Green for supporting examples
- ◆ Pink for details elaborating each example

The writing process:

1. Planning step (Outline)
2. Writing step (Organizer)
3. Editing step (Edited organizer)
4. Formatting step (Draft)
5. Publishing step (Final copy)

The editing process:

1. Save in the appropriate folder or directory.
2. Use text-to-speech to read and listen to each sentence, one at a time.
3. Check capitalization and punctuation.
4. Use transition words and a thesaurus, and vary sentence structure.
5. Read and listen.
6. Run spell checker.
7. Print in color and give to a proofreader to edit.

The Structured Writing Example Paragraph Process

The Planning Step

Students begin the planning step by opening the Inspiration template titled *Example Paragraph Web*, available on the accompanying CD-ROM. Discuss with your students the differences between the Reason Paragraph and Example Paragraph. Using the web view enhances understanding of the similarities and differences of these two paragraph types. The color code and the text help identify the essential elements of the paragraph: title, topic, three supporting **examples**, three details for each supporting **example**, and a conclusion.

Model the lesson by assigning an Example Paragraph on the topic: **"Fun on Vacation."**

1. The white box in the web indidcates a place for the student's name, the blue box is for the paragraph title, and the yellow boxes are for the topic and concluding ideas. The three green boxes below the topic signify the place for supporting **examples**. The three pink boxes will hold the details for each supporting **example**.

2. Students keyboard only single words and short phrases in the web to represent these examples. **Reinforce the concept of outlining as idea organization, not sentence writing**. The words and phrases will be converted into an outline to use as a guide for writing sentences in the organizer during the writing step of this process.

3. Students convert the web into a color-coded outline by selecting the outline option in Inspiration and running spell check to make initial spelling corrections. Inspiration's spell checker can be difficult for some students to use. If this problem arises, defer spell checking to the first editing step. Students save their outlines in the appropriate folder and directory.

Example Paragraph Web

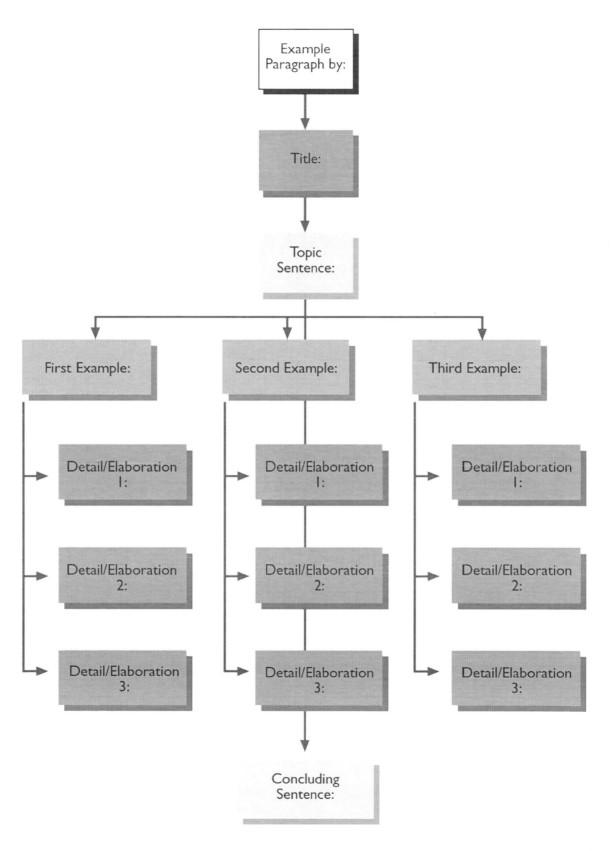

Example Paragraph Example

Example Paragraph by: **Student**

Title: **Fun on Vacation**

Topic Sentence: **three ways**

First Example: **bring a friend**

Second Example: **amusement park**

Third Example: **go to beach**

Detail/Elaboration 1: **like the same things**

Detail/Elaboration 2: **don't play with sister**

Detail/Elaboration 3: **play Gameboy**

Detail/Elaboration 1: **rides**

Detail/Elaboration 2: **junk food**

Detail/Elaboration 3: **buy souvenirs**

Detail/Elaboration 1: **swim/ boogie board**

Detail/Elaboration 2: **Frisbee**

Detail/Elaboration 3: **sand castles**

Concluding Sentence: **enjoy**

Example Paragraph Outline by:

I. Title:
   A. Topic Sentence:
      1. First Example:
         a. Detail/Elaboration 1:
         b. Detail/Elaboration 2:
         c. Detail/Elaboration 3:
      2. Second Example:
         a. Detail/Elaboration 1:
         b. Detail/Elaboration 2:
         c. Detail/Elaboration 3:
      3. Third Example:
         a. Detail/Elaboration 1:
         b. Detail/Elaboration 2:
         c. Detail/Elaboration 3:
   B. Concluding Sentence:

Example Paragraph Organizer by:

Title:
Topic Sentence:
First Example:
Detail/Elaboration 1:
Detail/Elaboration 2:
Detail/Elaboration 3:
Second Example:
Detail/Elaboration 1:
Detail/Elaboration 2:
Detail/Elaboration 3:
Third Example:
Detail/Elaboration 1:
Detail/Elaboration 2:
Detail/Elaboration 3:
Concluding Sentence:

4. Students print the color-coded outline and give it to the teacher, who checks the content and gives the students feedback. Reassured that the content is appropriate, students use this outline to continue with the next step of the writing process, the writing step.

The Writing Step

Students use the color-coded Structured Writing *Example Paragraph Organizer* and a word-processing program (Write:Outloud) as a guide to expand their examples from the outline into complete sentences in the organizer, one at a time.

Example Paragraph Outline by: Student

I. Title: Fun on Vacation
   A. Topic Sentence: three ways
      1. First Example: bring a friend
         a. Detail/Elaboration 1: like same things
         b. Detail/Elaboration 2: don't play with sister
         c. Detail/Elaboration 3: play gameboy
      2. Second Example: amusement park
         a. Detail/Elaboration 1: rides
         b. Detail/Elaboration 2: junk food
         c. Detail/Elaboration 3: buy souvenirs
      3. Third Example: go to beach
         a. Detail/Elaboration 1: swim/boogie board
         b. Detail/Elaboration 2: frisbee
         c. Detail/Elaboration 3: sand castles
   B. Concluding Sentence: enjoy

1. Using the outline as a guide, students write complete sentences in the organizer, one at a time. Each sentence will be revised and edited in the editing step, sentence by sentence.

2. Students expand and elaborate their sentences as they write. They compose sentences using the **examples** from their outlines that support their topic sentences. Teachers direct students to **use adjectives, adverbs, and prepositional phrases** to expand and clarify their writing, and to combine simple sentences into compound sentences.

3. Teachers should focus on **two new concepts** while teaching the Example Paragraph: **examples are the supporting sentences** requiring **three details** for each example. To make the detailed explanation clear, students identify these supporting examples by adding specific, **example transition words** that point the reader toward them. Teachers alert students to example transition words they can use. Posting these

Example Paragraph
Transition Words

- ▶ Each supporting idea is a new example
- ▶ Use **transitions** to separate supporting examples

- For example, another example, the last example
- The first example, the second example, the third example
- First of all, second, finally
- The first instance, the second instance, the third instance
- For instance
- Yet another example
- The final example

Example Paragraph Organizer by: Student

Title: Fun on Vacation
Topic Sentence: There are many ways to enjoy a vacation.
First Example: For example, invite a friend to go with you on your trip.
Detail/Elaboration 1: Make sure your friend likes to do the same things you do.
Detail/Elaboration 2: When you bring a friend, you don't have to always play with your sister.
Detail/Elaboration 3: You can also play your Gameboy with your friend.
Second Example: Second, kids love to visit an amusement park on vacation.
Detail/Elaboration 1: It is great fun to go on all the rides.
Detail/Elaboration 2: You get to eat lots of junk food at amusement parks.
Detail/Elaboration 3: It is fun to buy silly souvenirs.
Third Example: Finally, a trip to the beach is also enjoyable.
Detail/Elaboration 1: You can swim and boogie board at the beach.
Detail/Elaboration 2: People can play Frisbee on the beach.
Detail/Elaboration 3: It is also lots of fun to build sand castles and bury each other in the sand.
Concluding Sentence: These are some of the many ways to enjoy a vacation.

examples helps students use transition words with confidence.

4. Once all the sentences are completed, the students save the organizer appropriately in the proper folder or directory.

5. At this point, the teacher assesses the document for sentence structure and suggests expanding terms when appropriate.

The Editing Step

Students are required to use a specific editing process to make sure their sentences reflect what they mean to convey and to correct spelling and mechanical errors. This step becomes more complex as the students proceed through the Structured Writing sequence.

1. Students use text-to-speech to read and listen to each sentence, one at a time. Here, students add, delete, and change words until the sentences sound right and communicate what they mean.

2. Students check capitalization (the beginning of each sentence and proper nouns) and punctuation, word usage, and spelling. We recommend that students be taught to do this editing in the specific order. Using the spell checker in the word processor as the last step allows students a better chance to properly correct misspelled words.

3. Students make sure the three **examples** support the topic sentence, and that appropriate **transition words** indicate each supporting sentence or example. Students make sure the details elaborate each specific example.

4. During editing, after the initial structure, sequence, and purpose have been set, **students revise sentences to refine the paragraph.** These skills are taught only when the students are secure in

their ability to clearly write an example paragraph. Students need to **vary the structure of their sentences** (imperative, declarative, interrogatory, exclamatory), and **use the thesaurus** to develop a more complex vocabulary. **This expansion is not meant to increase creativity but to produce a more specific explanation of a concept.**

5. Students save the edited organizer in the proper folder or directory.

6. Teachers assess the sentences for structure, variation, the use of transition words, and proper syntax and give feedback to the students. Secure that syntax, grammar, spelling, and structure are correct, students move to the formatting step.

The Formatting Step

In this step, students remove the structure words from the organizer and put the sentence into paragraph form as a draft.

1. Students highlight the structure words and colons and delete them. As each structure word is deleted, students sequence the sentences one after the other paying attention to beginning capitalization, ending punctuation, and spacing between sentences and lines.

2. Under "name," students add the day's date and any other information that belongs in the heading.

3. Students center the title and check for proper capitalization.

4. Students indent the topic sentence.

5. Students read and listen again to the paragraph as a whole, assessing the flow and continuity of their paragraphs.

6. Students save the document as 'draft' in the proper folder or directory and print it out in color, providing a copy to a proofreader to edit.

Student
Date

Fun on Vacation

There are many ways to enjoy a vacation. For example, invite a friend to go with you on your trip. Make sure your friend likes to do the same things you do. When you bring a friend, you don't have to always play with your sister. You can also play your Gameboy with your friend. Secondly, kids love to visit an amusement park on vacation. It is great fun to go on all the rides. You get to eat lots of junk food at amusement parks. It is fun to buy silly souvenirs. Finally, a trip to the beach is also enjoyable. You can swim and boogie board at the beach. People can play Frisbee on the beach. It is also lots of fun to build sand castles and bury each other in the sand. These are some of the many ways to enjoy a vacation.

The Publishing Step

At this point, when students receive approved drafts, the writing process is completed except for removing the color and printing a final copy.

1. Students change the text color to black.

2. Students save the file in the appropriate folder or directory as *'final copy'* and print a final copy in black.

3. Students turn in a completed packet containing the outline, organizer, draft, and final copy.

In summary, the Structured Writing Example Paragraph modifies the Reason Paragraph by using:

♦ **Examples** as supporting sentences

♦ **Example** transition words

♦ Additional detail for each supporting sentence

Students must practice and master each new paragraph type before moving on to a more complex one. Teachers must be sure that students follow all the writing steps correctly. Visual reminders (posters) displayed throughout the classroom and kept in student binders make a good reference.

The writing process is the same throughout this program. Students follow the same process for each type of paragraph. The planning and outlining steps use Inspiration and teacher created webs. The writing step uses a word-processing program (Write:OutLoud) and teacher created organizers. The revising and editing steps follow the same sequence for all writing. The Structured Writing process culminates with the formatting and publishing steps. Though the paragraph types vary, the Structured Writing process and sequence remain the same.

As students write Example Paragraphs, they get practice expanding the number of sentences they write and increasing the complexity of the sentences. By assigning a topic for the Reason Paragraph and then rewriting it as an Example Paragraph, the difference between using reasons and examples to explain a concept is emphasized. Teachers continue to teach students how to vary sentence structure and use colorful adjectives and adverbs for more meaningful communication.

Suggested Topics for Example Paragraphs

- Things to do at recess
- Ways to annoy my brother or sister
- Summer jobs
- Interesting hobbies
- Kids' chores

- Favorite books, movies, television programs, etc.
- School sports
- Favorite desserts
- Healthy snacks
- Party games

Chapter 6

The Process Paragraph Lesson

Objectives:

1. Students will write a Process Paragraph using a title, a topic sentence, **supporting sentences that are the steps in a process sequenced in time order** with transition words to identify the steps in the process, **three detail sentences elaborating each step**, and a concluding sentence.

2. Students will learn the color codes, reinforcing the essential elements of the paragraph: blue for title, yellow for topic and concluding sentences, **green for sequenced steps in a process**, pink for details.

3. Students will use the steps of the Structured Writing process to plan, write, edit, and publish a Process Paragraph.

4. Students will use the sequential editing steps in Structured Writing. They will use text-to-speech features to read and listen while checking the writing content, capitalization and punctuation, and running the spell checker.

Materials needed:

1. Structured Writing CD-ROM

   a. Structured Writing Process Paragraph Web

   b. Structured Writing Process Paragraph Organizer

2. Inspiration 6.0

3. Word-processing program (Write:Outloud)

4. Paragraph Requirements poster (optional)

5. Editing Steps poster (optional)

6. Process Transition Words poster (optional)

Essential elements:

The Structured Writing process teaches students to write a Process Paragraph using:

1. A topic sentence

2. Supporting sentences that are **steps in a process**

3. **Three detail sentences** supporting each step

4. **Transition words to identify each step of a process**

5. A concluding sentence

Color codes:

- ◆ Blue for title
- ◆ Yellow for topic and concluding sentences
- ◆ Green for steps in a process
- ◆ Pink for details elaborating each step

The writing process:

1. Planning step (Outline)
2. Writing step (Organizer)
3. Editing step (Edited organizer)
4. Formatting step (Draft)
5. Publishing step (Final copy)

The editing process:

1. Save in the appropriate folder or directory.
2. Use text-to-speech to read and listen to each sentence, one at a time.
3. Check capitalization and punctuation.
4. Use transition words and a thesaurus, and vary sentence structure.
5. Read and listen.
6. Run spell checker.
7. Print in color and give to a proofreader to edit.

The Structured Writing Process Paragraph Procedure

The Planning Step

Students begin the planning step by opening the Inspiration template titled *Process Paragraph Web*, available on the accompanying CD-ROM. This template helps them organize their thoughts for writing. The color code and the text help identify the essential elements of the paragraph: title, topic, supporting sentences (steps in a process), three details for each supporting step, and a conclusion. Discuss with your students the differences between the Example Paragraph and the Process Paragraph. The Process Paragraph adds a required sequence to the support sentences as indicated by a change in the web view. Viewing the two structures together in web view helps students see the similarities and differences of the two paragraph types.

Model the lesson by assigning a process paragraph on the topic **"How to Make Peanut Butter."**

1. The white box in the web indicates a place to enter the student's name, the blue box is for the paragraph title, and the yellow boxes are for the topic and concluding ideas. The six green boxes below the topic sentence signify the place for specific steps in a process. The three pink boxes will hold the details for each supporting step.

2. Students keyboard only single words and short phrases in the web to represent the steps in a process (fill in all green boxes before going to the detail level). **Reinforce the concept of outlining as idea organization, not sentence writing.** The words and phrases will be converted into an outline to use as a guide for writing sentences in the organizer during the writing step of this process.

3. Students convert the web into a color-coded outline by selecting the outline option in Inspiration and running spell

Process Paragraph Web

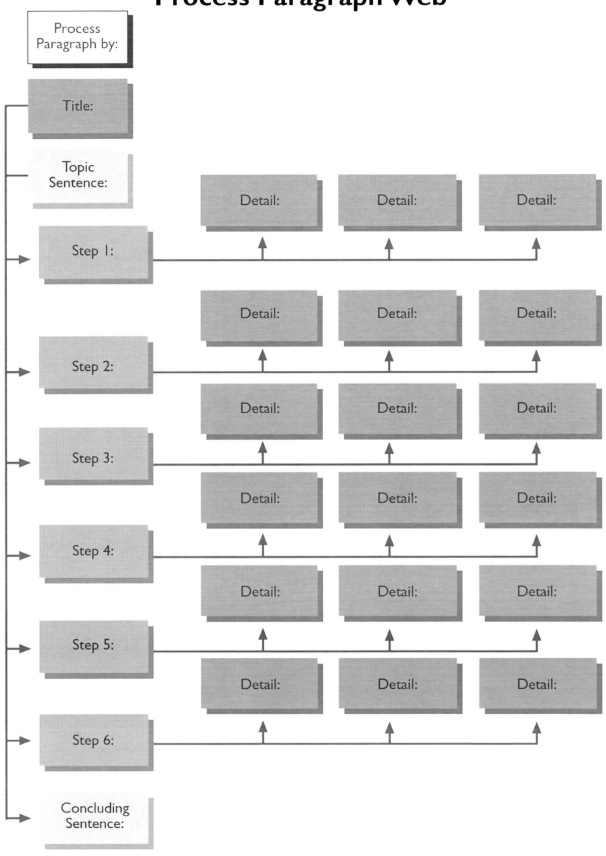

Process
Paragraph by:

Title:

Topic
Sentence:

Step 1:

Detail: Detail: Detail:

Step 2:

Detail: Detail: Detail:

Detail: Detail: Detail:

Step 3:

Detail: Detail: Detail:

Step 4:

Detail: Detail: Detail:

Step 5:

Detail: Detail: Detail:

Step 6:

Concluding
Sentence:

Process Paragraph Example

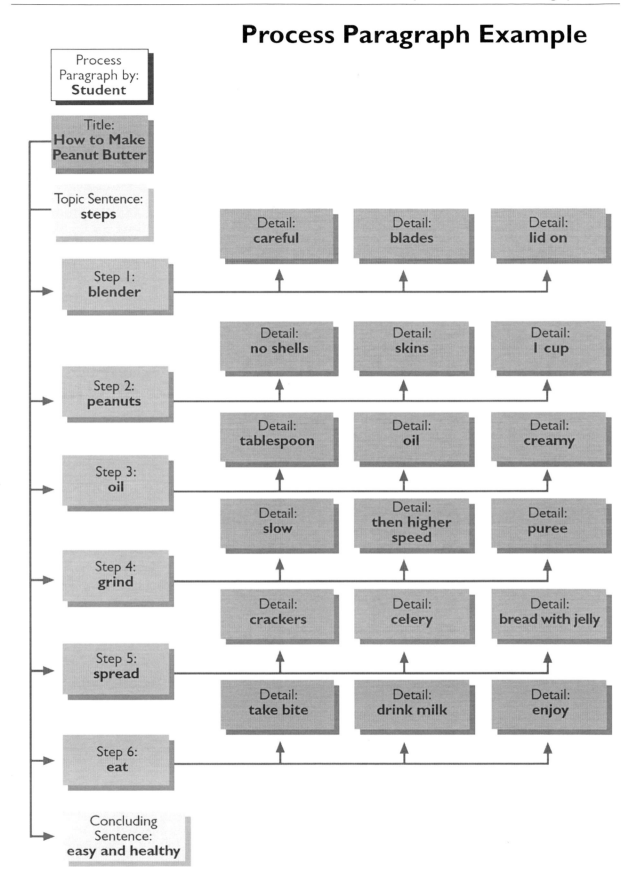

Process Paragraph by: **Student**

Title: **How to Make Peanut Butter**

Topic Sentence: **steps**

Step 1: **blender**

Detail: **careful**

Detail: **blades**

Detail: **lid on**

Step 2: **peanuts**

Detail: **no shells**

Detail: **skins**

Detail: **1 cup**

Step 3: **oil**

Detail: **tablespoon**

Detail: **oil**

Detail: **creamy**

Step 4: **grind**

Detail: **slow**

Detail: **then higher speed**

Detail: **puree**

Step 5: **spread**

Detail: **crackers**

Detail: **celery**

Detail: **bread with jelly**

Step 6: **eat**

Detail: **take bite**

Detail: **drink milk**

Detail: **enjoy**

Concluding Sentence: **easy and healthy**

Process Paragraph Outline by:

I. Title:
   A. Topic Sentence:
     1. Step 1:
       a. Detail 1:
       b. Detail 2:
       c. Detail 3:
     2. Step 2:
       a. Detail 1:
       b. Detail 2:
       c. Detail 3:
     3. Step 3:
       a. Detail 1:
       b. Detail 2:
       c. Detail 3:
     4. Step 4:
       a. Detail 1:
       b. Detail 2:
       c. Detail 3:
     5. Step 5:
       a. Detail 1:
       b. Detail 2:
       c. Detail 3:
     6. Step 6:
       a. Detail 1:
       b. Detail 2:
       c. Detail 3:
   B. Concluding Sentence:

Process Paragraph Organizer by:

Title:
Topic Sentence:
Step 1:
Detail 1:
Detail 2:
Detail 3:
Second Step:
Detail 1:
Detail 2:
Detail 3:
Third Step:
Detail 1:
Detail 2:
Detail 3:
Fourth Step:
Detail 1:
Detail 2:
Detail 3:
Fifth Step:
Detail 1:
Detail 2:
Detail 3:
Sixth Step:
Detail 1:
Detail 2:
Detail 3:
Concluding Sentence:

check to make initial spelling corrections. Inspiration's spell checker can be difficult for some students to use. If this problem arises, defer spell checking to the first editing step. Students save their outlines in the appropriate folder or directory.

4. Students print the color-coded outline and give it to the teacher, who checks the content and gives the students feedback. Reassured that the content is appropriate, students use this outline to continue with the next step of the writing process, the writing step.

The Writing Step

Students use the color-coded Structured Writing *Process Paragraph Organizer* and a word-processing program (Write:Outloud) to guide and expand their examples from the outline into complete sentences in the organizer, one at a time.

1. Using the outline as a guide, students create complete sentences in the organizer, one at a time. Each sentence will be revised and edited in the editing step, sentence by sentence.

2. Students expand and elaborate their sentences as they write. **They compose sentences using sequenced steps in a**

Process Paragraph

Transition Words

- ▶ Each supporting idea is a new step
- ▶ Use **transitions** to separate supporting steps

- To begin with
- The first/second/third/.../step
- At this point
- Next
- Finally
- Then
- Also
- When
- The final/last step
- At last

Process Paragraph Outline by: Student

I. Title: How to Make Peanut Butter
  A. Topic Sentence: steps
    1. Step 1: blender
      a. Detail 1: careful
      b. Detail 2: sharp blades
      c. Detail 3: lid on
    2. Step 2: peanuts
      a. Detail 1: no shells
      b. Detail 2: no skins
      c. Detail 3: 1 cup
    3. Step 3: oil
      a. Detail 1: 1 tablespoon
      b. Detail 2: peanut oil
      c. Detail 3: makes creamy
    4. Step 4: grind
      a. Detail 1: slow
      b. Detail 2: then higher speed
      c. Detail 3: puree
    5. Step 5: spread
      a. Detail 1: crackers
      b. Detail 2: celery
      c. Detail 3: bread with jelly
    6. Step 6: eat
      a. Detail 1: take bite
      b. Detail 2: drink milk
      c. Detail 3: enjoy
  B. Concluding Sentence: easy and healthy

process. Teachers direct students to use adjectives, adverbs, and prepositional phrases to expand and clarify their writing, and to combine simple sentences into compound sentences.

3. Teachers focus on **two new concepts** while teaching the Process Paragraph: **steps in a process are the supporting sentences**, which require three details for each step, and the **Process Paragraph web is in a vertical, sequential form.** To make the detailed explanation clear, students identify these sequenced steps by adding transition words that point the reader toward them. Teachers alert students to sequential transition words they can use. Posting these samples helps students use transition words with confidence.

4. Once all the sentences are completed, the students save the organizer in the proper folder or directory.

5. At this point, the teacher assesses the document for sentence structure and suggests expanding terms when appropriate.

The Editing Step

Students are required to use a specific editing process to make sure their sentences reflect what they meant to convey and to correct spelling and mechanical errors. This step becomes more complex as the students proceed through the Structured Writing sequence.

1. Students use text-to-speech to read and listen to each sentence, one at a time. Here, students add, delete, and change words until the sentences sound right and communicate what they mean.

2. Students check capitalization (the beginning of each sentence and proper nouns) and punctuation, word usage, and spelling. We recommend that students be taught to do this editing in the specific order. Using the spell checker in the word processor as the last step gives students a better chance to properly correct misspelled words.

3. Students make sure the steps of the process (supporting sentences) are **sequenced in a specific time order** to support the topic sentence, and that appropriate transition words indicate each supporting sentence or step in a process.

Process Paragraph Organizer by: Student

Title: How to Make Peanut Butter
Topic Sentence: Peanut butter is easy to make if you follow a few simple steps.
First Step: To begin with, you need a blender that works well.
Detail 1: Be careful because the blender's blades are very sharp.
Detail 2: If the blender's blades are dull, get better ones or the peanut butter won't be as creamy.
Detail 3: Be sure to put the lid on or the peanuts will fly all over the room and make a big mess.
Second Step: Secondly, you need to grind the peanuts in the blender.
Detail 1: You need to take the shells off the peanuts or your peanut butter will be very crunchy.
Detail 2: You also need to take the skins off the peanuts or there will be tough spots in your peanut butter.
Detail 3: You use one cup of shelled and skinned peanuts for this recipe.
Third Step: Next, add the oil to the peanuts in the blender.
Detail 1: Use one tablespoon of oil with one cup of peanuts.
Detail 2: Peanut oil works the best.
Detail 3: The oil makes the peanut butter creamy.
Fourth Step: Then, grind the peanuts and oil in the blender.
Detail 1: You should start on a slow speed to mix the ingredients first.
Detail 2: After it is mixed, speed it up to puree.
Detail 3: Keep it at puree until it gets smooth and creamy.
Fifth Step: At this point, the peanut butter is ready to spread.
Detail 1: You can spread it on graham crackers with honey for 'tiger' snacks.
Detail 2: Spread peanut butter on celery with raisins for 'ants on a log.'
Detail 3: Spread it on bread with jelly and you have my favorite snack.
Sixth Step: Finally, you are ready to eat the peanut butter.
Detail 1: Spread the peanut butter to make your favorite snack and take a big bite and swallow.
Detail 2: "Got milk?" If you don't, you need to get some or you will have peanut butter stuck to the roof of your mouth for a long time.
Detail 3: Savor the fresh, peanut taste.
Concluding Sentence: Enjoy your healthy peanut butter snack but don't forget the milk!

4. During editing, after the initial structure, sequence, and purpose have been set, students revise sentences to refine the paragraph. These skills are taught only when the students are secure in their ability to clearly write a process paragraph. Students need to vary the structure of their sentences (imperative, declarative, interrogatory, exclamatory), and use the thesaurus to develop a more complex vocabulary. This expansion is not meant to increase creativity but to produce a more specific explanation of a concept.

5. Students save the edited organizer in the appropriate folder or directory.

6. Teachers assess the sentences for structure, variation, use of transition words, and proper syntax to give feedback to the students. Secure that syntax, grammar, spelling, and structure are correct, students move to the formatting step.

The Formatting Step

In this step, students remove the structure words from the organizer and put the sentences into paragraph form as a draft.

1. Students highlight the structure words and colons and delete them. As each structure word is deleted, students sequence the sentences one after the other, paying attention to beginning capitalization, ending punctuation, and spacing between sentences and lines.

2. Under "name," students add the day's date and any other information that belongs in the heading.

Student
Date

How to Make Peanut Butter

Peanut butter is easy to make if you follow a few simple steps. To begin with, you need a blender that works well. Be careful because the blender's blades are very sharp. If the blender's blades are dull, get better ones or the peanut butter won't be as creamy. Be sure to put the lid on or the peanuts will fly all over the room and make a big mess. Secondly, you need to grind the peanuts in the blender. You need to take the shells off the peanuts or your peanut butter will be very crunchy. You also need to take the skins off the peanuts or there will be tough spots in your peanut butter. You use one cup of shelled and skinned peanuts for this recipe. Next, add the oil to the peanuts in the blender. Use one tablespoon of oil with one cup of peanuts. Peanut oil works the best. The oil makes the peanut butter creamy. Then, grind the peanuts and oil in the blender. You should start on a slow speed to mix the ingredients first. After it is mixed, speed it up to puree. Keep it at puree until it gets smooth and creamy. At this point, the peanut butter is ready to spread. You can spread it on graham crackers with honey for 'tiger' snacks. Spread peanut butter on celery with raisins for 'ants on a log.' Spread it on bread with jelly and you have my favorite snack. Finally, you are ready to eat the peanut butter. Spread the peanut butter to make your favorite snack and take a big bite and swallow. "Got milk?" If you don't, you need to get some or you will have peanut butter stuck to the roof of your mouth for a long time. Savor the fresh, peanut taste. Enjoy your healthy peanut butter snack but don't forget the milk!

---

3. Students center the title and check for proper capitalization.

4. Students indent the topic sentence.

5. Students read and listen again to the paragraph as a whole, paying particular attention to the sequence of steps to ensure that the process makes sense.

6. Students save the document as *'draft'* in the appropriate folder or directory and print it out in color, providing a copy to a proofreader to edit.

The Publishing Step

At this point, when students receive approved drafts, the writing process is completed except for removing the color and printing a final copy.

1. Students change the text color to black.

2. Students save the file in the appropriate folder or directory as *'final copy'* and print a final copy in black.

3. Students submit a complete packet containing the outline, organizer, draft, and final copy.

In summary, the Structure Writing Process Paragraph modifies the previously taught paragraphs (Basic, Expanded, Reason, and Example) by using:

♦ **Steps in a process** as supporting sentences

♦ Transition words to identify supporting steps

♦ Supporting sentences that have a **sequential time order**

♦ A thesaurus to replace generic words with more complex vocabulary

Students should now be comfortable with the process used for Structured Writing. It may be necessary to reinforce the process if students start to take shortcuts. Teachers can now emphasize content and complexity, allowing the built-in structure of the process to reinforce the essential elements of the paragraph type being taught. The next step in the paragraph progression is to write paragraphs that classify objects and ideas.

The writing process is the same throughout this program. Students follow the same process for each type of paragraph. The planning and outlining steps use Inspiration and teacher-created webs. The writing step uses a word-processing program (Write:OutLoud) and teacher-created organizers. The revising and editing steps follow the same sequence for all writing. The Structured Writing process culminates with the formatting and publishing steps. Though the paragraph types vary, the Structured Writing process and sequence remain the same.

Suggested Topics for Process Paragraphs

- Snacks (recipes) I can make
- Planning a birthday party
- Washing the dog
- Making a peanut butter and jelly sandwich

- Building a snowman
- Decorating a Christmas tree
- Building a model

Chapter 7

The Classification Paragraph Lesson

Objectives:

1. Students will write a Classification Paragraph using a title, a topic sentence, three supporting sentences using **categories** with **transition words, three detail sentences elaborating or defining each supporting category**, and a concluding sentence.

2. Students will learn the color codes, reinforcing the essential elements of the paragraph: blue for title, yellow for topic and concluding sentences, green for supporting **categories**, pink for details about each category.

3. Students will use the steps of the Structured Writing process to plan, write, edit, and publish a Classification Paragraph.

4. Students will use the sequential editing steps in Structured Writing. They will use text-to-speech features to read and listen while checking the writing content, capitalization and punctuation, and running the spell checker.

Materials needed:

1. Structured Writing CD-ROM

   a. Structured Writing Classification Paragraph Web

   b. Structured Writing Classification Paragraph Organizer

2. Inspiration 6.0

3. Word-processing program (Write:Outloud)

4. Paragraph Requirements poster (optional)

5. Editing Steps poster (optional)

6. Classification Transition Words poster (optional)

Essential elements:

The Structured Writing process teaches students to write a Classification Paragraph using:

1. A topic sentence

2. Three supporting sentences using **categories**

3. **Three detail sentences supporting** each category

4. Transition words for each supporting category

5. A concluding sentence

Color codes:

- ◆ Blue for title
- ◆ Yellow for topic and concluding sentences
- ◆ Green for supporting categories
- ◆ Pink for examples and details elaborating each class or category

The writing process:

1. Planning step (Outline)
2. Writing step (Organizer)
3. Editing step (Edited organizer)
4. Formatting step (Draft)
5. Publishing step (Final copy)

The editing process:

1. Save in the appropriate folder or directory.
2. Use text-to-speech to read and listen to each sentence, one at a time.
3. Check capitalization and punctuation.
4. Use transition words and a thesaurus, and vary sentence structure.
5. Read and listen.
6. Run spell checker.
7. Print in color and give to a proofreader to edit.

The Structured Writing Classification Paragraph Process

The Planning Step

Students begin the planning step by opening the Inspiration template titled *Classification Paragraph Web*, available on the accompanying CD-ROM. This template helps them organize their thoughts for writing. The color code and the text help identify the essential elements of the paragraph: title, topic, three supporting **categories, three** details and examples for each supporting **category**, and a conclusion.

The teacher should point out the similarities in structure between the Reason, Example, and Classification Paragraphs and discuss how the primary difference is the type of supporting sentences. For the Classification Paragraph, we use categories or groups as supporting sentences. Along with details, we use examples of each group to more clearly define the category. Comparing the web forms of these paragraphs helps students identify both the similarities in structure and the differences in types of supporting sentences.

Model the lesson by assigning a Classification Paragraph on the topic **"Breakfast Foods."**

1. The white box in the web indicates a place for the student's name, the blue box is for the paragraph title, and the yellow boxes are for the topic and concluding ideas. The three green boxes below the topic sentence signify the place for supporting **categories**. The three pink boxes will hold the details for each **category**.

2. Students keyboard only single words and short phrases in the web to represent these categories. **Reinforce the concept of outlining as idea organization, not sentence writing.** The words and phrases will be converted into an outline to use as a guide for writing

Classification Paragraph Web

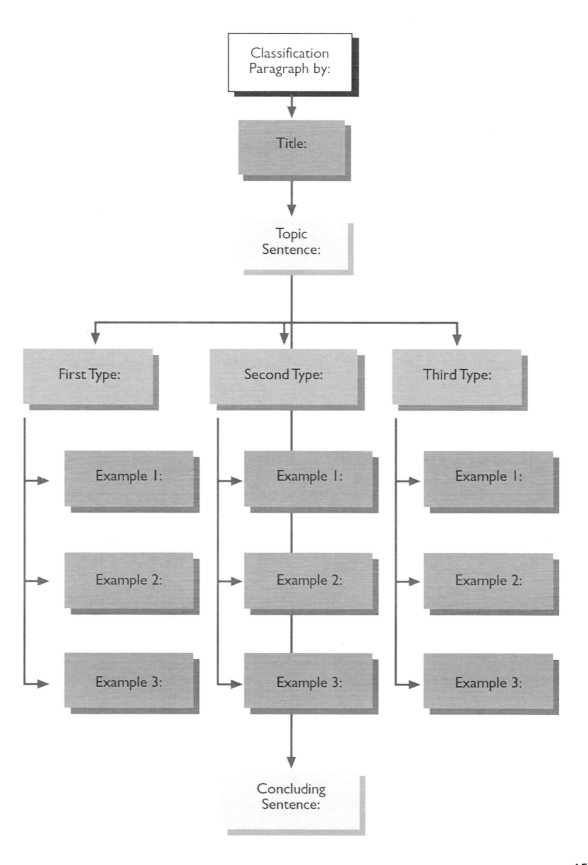

Classification
Paragraph by:

Title:

Topic
Sentence:

First Type:

Second Type:

Third Type:

Example 1:

Example 1:

Example 1:

Example 2:

Example 2:

Example 2:

Example 3:

Example 3:

Example 3:

Concluding
Sentence:

Classification Paragraph Example

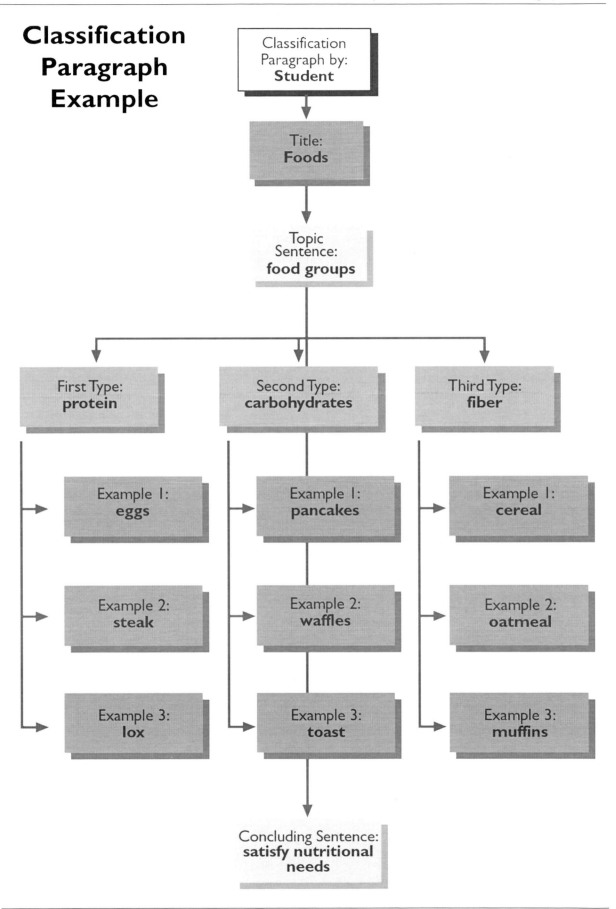

Classification Paragraph by: **Student**

Title: **Foods**

Topic Sentence: **food groups**

First Type: **protein**

Second Type: **carbohydrates**

Third Type: **fiber**

Example 1: **eggs**

Example 1: **pancakes**

Example 1: **cereal**

Example 2: **steak**

Example 2: **waffles**

Example 2: **oatmeal**

Example 3: **lox**

Example 3: **toast**

Example 3: **muffins**

Concluding Sentence: **satisfy nutritional needs**

Classification Paragraph Outline by:	Classification Paragraph Organizer by:
I. Title:	Title:
A. Topic Sentence:	Topic Sentence:
1. First Type:	First Type:
a. Example 1:	Example 1:
b. Example 2:	Example 2:
c. Example 3:	Example 3:
2. Second Type:	Second Type:
a. Example 1:	Example 1:
b. Example 2:	Example 2:
c. Example 3:	Example 3:
3. Third Type:	Third Type:
a. Example 1:	Example 1:
b. Example 2:	Example 2:
c. Example 3:	Example 3:
B. Concluding Sentence:	Concluding Sentence:

sentences in the organizer during the writing step of this process.

3. Students convert the web into a color-coded outline by selecting the outline option in Inspiration and running spell check to make initial spelling corrections. Inspiration's spell checker can be difficult for some students to use. If this problem arises, defer spell checking to the first editing step. Students save their outlines in the appropriate folder or directory.

4. Students print the color-coded outline and give it to the teacher, who checks the content and gives the students feedback. Reassured that the content is appropriate, students use this outline to continue with the next step, the writing step.

The Writing Step

Students use the color-coded Structured Writing *Classification Paragraph Organizer* and a word-processing program (Write:Outloud) to guide and expand their

ideas from the outline into complete sentences in the organizer, one at a time.

1. Using the outline as a guide, students create complete sentences in the organizer, one at a time. Each sentence will be revised and edited in the editing step, sentence by sentence.

2. Students expand and elaborate their sentences as they write. Teachers direct students to **use adjectives, adverbs, and prepositional phrases** to expand and clarify their writing, and to combine simple sentences into compound sentences.

3. Teachers should focus on **a single new concept** while writing the Classification Paragraph: **categories are the supporting sentences.** To make the detailed explanation clear, students identify these supporting categories by adding specific classification **transition words** to point the reader toward them. Teachers alert students to the different transition words they can use. Posting these examples helps students use transition words with confidence.

4. Once all the sentences are completed, the students save the organizer in the proper folder or directory.

5. At this point, the teacher assesses the document for sentence structure and suggests expanding terms when appropriate.

The Editing Step

Students are required to use a specific editing process to make sure their sentences reflect what they meant to convey and to correct spelling and mechanical errors. This step becomes more complex as the students proceed through the Structured Writing sequence.

1. Students use text-to-speech to read and listen to each sentence, one at a time. Here, students add, delete, and change words until the sentences sound right and communicate what they mean.

2. Students check capitalization (the beginning of each sentence and proper nouns) and punctuation, word usage, and spelling. We recommend that students be taught to do this editing in the specific order. Using the spell checker in the word processor as the last step allows students a better chance to properly correct misspelled words.

3. Students make sure that **three categories** support the topic sentence, and that appropriate **transition words** indicate each supporting category or classification. Students check to ensure details elaborate and define each specific classification.

4. During editing, after the initial structure, sequence, and purpose have been set, students then revise sentences to refine the paragraph. These skills are taught only when the students are secure in their ability to clearly write a Classification Paragraph. Students need

---

Classification Paragraph
Transition Words

▶ Each supporting idea is a new category

▶ Use **transitions** to separate the categories

- The first/the second/the third
- One kind/another kind
- One type of/another type of
- The best/the worst type or kind
- The last type or kind

Classification Paragraph Outline by: Student

I. Title: Breakfast Foods
  A. Topic Sentence: food groups
    1. First Type: protein
      a. Example 1: eggs
      b. Example 2: steak
      c. Example 3: lox
    2. Second Type: carbohydrates
      a. Example 1: pancakes
      b. Example 2: waffles
      c. Example 3: french toast
    3. Third Type: fiber
      a. Example 1: cold cereal
      b. Example 2: oatmeal
      c. Example 3: muffins
  B. Concluding Sentence: satisfy nutritional needs

to **vary the structure of their sentences** (imperative, declarative, interrogatory, exclamatory), and **use the thesaurus** to develop a more complex vocabulary. **This expansion is not meant to increase creativity but to produce a more specific explanation of a concept.**

5. Students save the edited organizer in the proper folder or directory.

6. Teachers assess the sentences for structure, variation, the use of transition words, and proper syntax to give feedback to the students. Secure that syntax, grammar, spelling, and structure are correct, students then move to the formatting step.

The Formatting Step

In this step, students remove the structure words from the organizer and put the sentences into paragraph form as a draft.

1. Students highlight the structure words and colons and delete them. As each structure word is deleted, students sequence the sentences one after the other, paying attention to beginning capitalization, ending punctuation, and spacing between sentences and lines.

2. Under "name," students add the day's date and any other information that belongs in the heading.

3. Students center the title and check words for proper capitalization.

4. Students indent the topic sentence.

5. Students read and listen again to the paragraph as a whole, assessing the flow and continuity of their paragraphs.

6. Students save the document as *'draft'* in the proper file or directory and print it out in color, providing a copy to a proofreader to edit.

The Publishing Step

At this point, when students receive approved drafts, the writing process is completed except for removing the color and printing a final copy.

1. Students change the text color to black.

2. Students save the file in the appropriate file or directory as *'final copy'* and print a final copy in black.

3. Students submit a complete packet containing the outline, organizer, draft, and final copy.

In summary, the Classification Paragraph expands the concept for paragraph writing by:

- ◆ Using more than one idea or object as the central subject of the paragraph

- ◆ Using categories or groupings of different objects or ideas as supporting sentences (using a broader frame of reference than in Reason or Example Paragraphs)

- ◆ Adding transition words to identify the categories

- ◆ Using details as examples of each category or group

The writing process is the same throughout this program. Students follow the same process for each type of paragraph. The planning and outlining steps use Inspiration and teacher-created templates. The writing step uses a word-processing program (Write:OutLoud) and teacher-created templates. The revising and editing steps follow the same sequence for all paragraphs. The Structured Writing process culminates with the formatting and publishing steps. Though the paragraph types vary, the Structured Writing process and sequence remain the same.

Students must practice and master each new paragraph type before moving on to a more complex one. Teachers must be sure that students follow all the writing steps correctly. Visual reminders (posters) displayed throughout the classroom and kept

Student
Date

Breakfast Foods

Breakfast foods can be classified according to the amount of a basic food group that they contain. One category of breakfast foods is made up mainly of protein. Eggs cooked in a variety of ways from soft boiled to scrambled are high in protein. Steak is oftentimes combined with eggs to make a meal even higher in protein. Lox, or raw salmon, is another example of a breakfast food high in protein. A second type of breakfast food is primarily comprised of carbohydrates. Pancakes with syrup have a high measure of carbohydrates. Waffles with fruit or jam are also mainly comprised of carbohydrates. French toast is another breakfast food made from bread and usually garnished with powdered sugar or another sweet topping that is rich in carbohydrates. A third type of breakfast food is one that is basically high in fiber. Cold cereals made from wheat, bran and other grains are full of fiber. Hot cereals such as oatmeal, Cream of Wheat and Cream of Rice are made up of foods rich in fiber. Muffins and breads made from grains are complex carbohydrates high in fiber. One's choice of breakfast foods can often satisfy a body's need for protein, carbohydrate, or fiber in a person's diet.

in student binders make a good reference. Students must write several different Classification Paragraphs before moving on to the more difficult Compare and Contrast Paragraph.

Suggested Topics for Classification Paragraphs

- Vacations: summer, fall, winter, spring; adventure, educational, or relaxation vacations; family, adult, child vacations

- Types of movies: dramas, comedies, adventure

- Schools: elementary, middle, high; private, public, and non-public schools

- Dogs: breeds; sizes; working or pets

- Sports: team, individual; contact, non-contact; high school, college, professional; Olympic events; types of equipment needed

- Transportation: airplanes, trains, automobiles, ships

- Food: healthy, junk; sweet, sour, hot, spicy, salty; breakfast, lunch, dinner, snacks, desserts

Chapter 8

The Compare and Contrast Paragraph Lesson

This paragraph compares and contrasts two items or ideas. We use the term "compare" to illustrate similarities between two entities, and the term "contrast" to focus on the differences between two entities. We start by using a comparison of two items for beginning Compare Paragraphs. We think this is an easier concept to work with for the students. After writing several Compare Paragraphs, we introduce a paragraph contrasting two items. Later, students mix comparison and contrast in a single paragraph when they are comfortable with the structure.

Objectives:

1. Students will write a Compare and Contrast Paragraph using a title, a topic sentence identifying **two items to be compared in order, three points of comparison** as supporting sentences with transition words to identify them, **two detail sentences** (one about each item **in specific order** with regard to the point of comparison), and a concluding sentence.

2. Students will use the color codes, reinforcing the essential elements of the paragraph: blue for title, yellow for topic and concluding sentences, green for supporting points of comparison, pink for details about each item in specific order.

3. Students will use the steps of the Structured Writing process to plan, write, edit, and publish a Compare and Contrast Paragraph.

4. Students will use the sequential editing steps in Structured Writing. They will use text-to-speech features to read and listen while checking the writing content, capitalization and punctuation, and running the spell checker.

Materials needed:

1. Structured Writing CD-ROM

    a. Structured Writing Comparison and Contrast Paragraph Web

    b. Structured Writing Comparison and Contrast Paragraph Organizer

2. Inspiration 6.0

3. Word-processing program (Write:Outloud)

4. Paragraph Requirements poster (optional)

5. Editing Steps poster (optional)

6. Compare and Contrast Transition Words poster (optional)

Essential elements:

The Structured Writing process teaches students to write a Compare and Contrast Paragraph using:

1. A topic sentence

2. **Three points of comparison** as supporting sentences

3. Two detail sentences, one about each point of comparison **in specific order**

4. Transition words used to identify **each point of comparison**

5. A concluding sentence

Color codes:

♦ Blue for title

♦ Yellow for topic and concluding sentences

♦ Green for supporting **points of comparison**

♦ Pink for each of the items elaborating the point of comparison

The writing process:

1. Planning step (Outline)

2. Writing step (Organizer)

3. Editing step (Edited organizer)

4. Formatting step (Draft)

5. Publishing step (Final copy)

The editing process:

1. Save in the appropriate folder or directory.

2. Use text-to-speech to read and listen to each sentence, one at a time.

3. Check capitalization and punctuation.

4. Use transition words and a thesaurus, and vary sentence structure.

5. Read and listen.

6. Run Spell checker.

7. Print in color and give to a proofreader to edit.

The Structured Writing Compare Paragraph Process

We teach students to write Compare and Contrast Paragraphs in three steps. First, we use points of comparison to compare motorcycles and bicycles. When students have successfully completed a Compare Paragraph, we use points of difference to contrast motorcycles and bicycles. Having completed a successful Contrast Paragraph, we then mix points of comparison and contrast to write a paragraph that compares and contrasts motorcycles and bicycles.

The Planning Step

Students begin the planning step by opening the Inspiration template titled *Compare and Contrast Paragraph Web*, available on the accompanying CD-ROM. The color code and the text help identify the essential elements of the paragraph: title, topic, three supporting ideas, and a conclusion. The color code and the text help identify the essential elements of the paragraph: title,

Compare and Contrast Paragraph Web

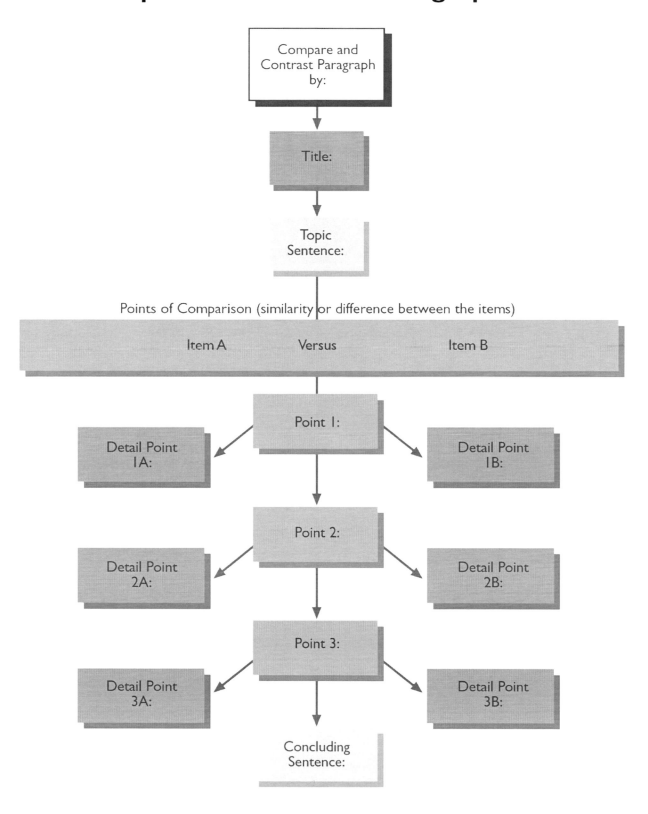

Compare and Contrast Paragraph by:

Title:

Topic Sentence:

Points of Comparison (similarity or difference between the items)

Item A   Versus   Item B

Point 1:

Detail Point 1A: Detail Point 1B:

Point 2:

Detail Point 2A: Detail Point 2B:

Point 3:

Detail Point 3A: Detail Point 3B:

Concluding Sentence:

topic sentence, three supporting points of comparison, two details elaborating the point of comparison for each of the items in order, and a conclusion.

Model the lesson by assigning a Compare Paragraph on the topic **"Motorcycles and Bicycles."**

1. The white box in the web indicates a place for the student's name, the blue box for the paragraph title, and the yellow boxes for the topic and concluding ideas. **The horizontal green box indicates Item A and Item B for the place and order of the two items to be compared. Item A will always be referred to before Item B in the supporting sentences.** The center vertical positioning of each point of comparison (structure sentences-green) indicates that there are two sides of details for each. The two pink boxes signal the place for the details elaborating each point for the items.

2. Students keyboard only single words and short phrases in the web to represent these comparisons. **Reinforce the concept of outlining as idea organization, not sentence writing.** The words

and phrases will be converted into an outline and used as a guide for writing sentences in the organizer during the writing step.

3. Students convert the web into a color-coded outline by selecting the outline option in Inspiration and running spell check to make initial spelling corrections. Inspiration's spell checker can be difficult for some students to use. If this problem arises, defer spell checking to the first editing step. Students save their outlines in the appropriate folder or directory.

4. Students print the color-coded outline and give it to the teacher, who checks the content and gives the students feedback. Reassured that the content is appropriate, students use this outline to continue with the writing step.

The Writing Step

Students use the color-coded Structured Writing *Comparison and Contrast Paragraph Organizer* and a word-processing program (Write:Outloud) as a guide to

Compare Paragraph Outline by:	Compare Paragraph Organizer by:

I. Title:
    A. Topic Sentence:
    Points of Comparison
    Item A: Versus   Item B:
        1. Point 1:
            a. Detail Point 1A:
            b. Detail Point 1B:
        2. Point 2:
            a. Detail Point 2A:
            b. Detail Point 2B:
        3. Point 3:
            a. Detail Point 3A:
            b. Detail Point 3B:
    B. Concluding Sentence:
	Title:
	Topic Sentence:
	Point of Comparison 1:
	Detail Point 1A:
	Detail Point 1B:
	Point of Comparison 2:
	Detail Point 2A:
	Detail Point 2B:
	Point of Comparison 3:
	Detail Point 3A:
	Detail Point 3B:
	Concluding Sentence:

Compare Paragraph Example

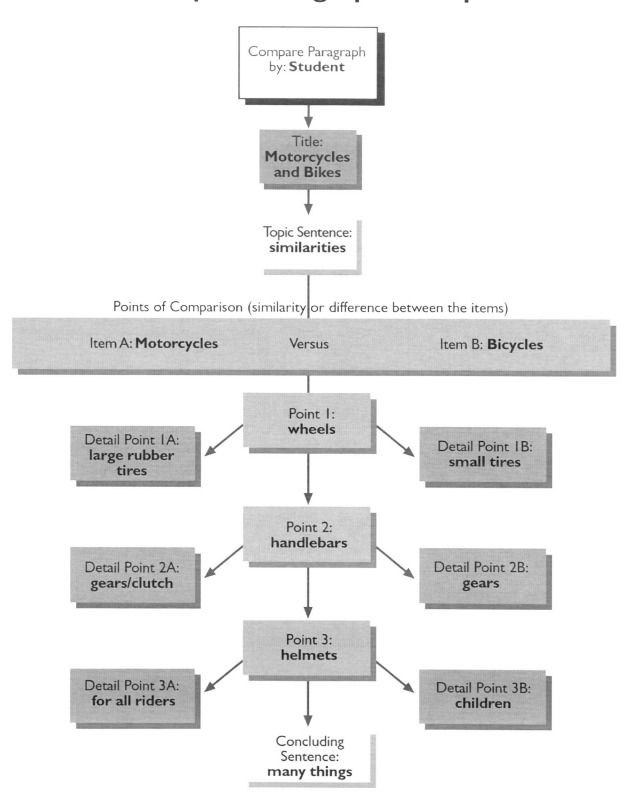

expand their ideas from the outline into complete sentences in the organizer, one at a time.

1. Using the outline as a guide, students write complete sentences in the organizer, one at a time. Each sentence will be revised and edited in the editing step, sentence by sentence.

2. Students expand and elaborate their sentences as they write. Teachers direct students **to use adjectives, adverbs, and prepositional phrases** to expand and clarify their writing, and to combine simple sentences into compound sentences.

3. Teachers should focus on **two new concepts** while teaching the Compare Paragraph.

   • First, **points of comparison are the supporting sentences.** To make the detailed explanation clear, students identify these supporting points of comparison by adding specific, comparison transition words to direct the reader toward them. Teachers alert students to the different transition words they can use. Posting these examples helps stu-

dents use transition words with confidence.

   • Second, **the details elaborate the points of comparison for each item in a specific order.** Each detail sentence explains that item (A, then B) with regard to the point of comparison.

4. Once all the sentences are completed, the students save the organizer in the proper folder or directory.

5. At this point, the teacher assesses the document for sentence structure and suggests expanding terms when appropriate.

The Editing Step

Students are required to use a specific editing process to make sure their sentences reflect what they meant to convey and to correct spelling and mechanical errors. This step becomes more complex as the students proceed through the Structured Writing sequence.

1. Students use text-to-speech to read and listen to each sentence, one at a time.

Compare Paragraph Outline by: Student

I. Title: Motorcycles and Bicycles
    A. Topic Sentence: similarities
    Points of Comparison (similarity or difference between the items)
    Item A: Motorcycles   **Versus**   **Item B:** Bicycles
    1. Point 1: two wheels
        a. Detail Point 1A: large rubber tires
        b. Detail Point 1B: small tires
    2. Point 2: handlebars
        a. Detail Point 2A: gears/clutch
        b. Detail Point 2B: gears
    3. Point 3: helmets
        a. Detail Point 3A: for all riders
        b. Detail Point 3B: children
    B. Concluding Sentence: many things in common

Compare and Contrast Paragraph
Transition Words

▸ Each supporting idea is a point of comparison

▸ Use **transitions** to separate points of comparison

• Both	• By contrast
• Also	• On the other hand
• Likewise	
• Have in common	• Unlike
	• Instead of
• Share the same	• But
	• Another difference
• Another likeness	

Here, students add, delete, and change words until the sentences sound right and communicate what they mean.

2. Students check capitalization (the beginning of each sentence and proper nouns) and punctuation, word usage, and spelling. We recommend that students be taught to do this editing in the specific order. Using the spell checker in the word processor as the last step allows students a better chance to properly correct misspelled words.

3. Students make sure that **three points of comparison** support the topic sentence, and that appropriate transition words indicate each point of comparison. Students check to ensure details elaborate each specific point of comparison **with items in the proper order**.

4. During editing, after the initial structure, sequence, and purpose have been set, students revise the sentences to refine the paragraph. These skills are taught only when the students are secure in their ability to clearly write a Compare Paragraph. Students need to **vary the structure of their sentences** (imperative, declarative, interrogatory, exclamatory), and **use the thesaurus** to develop a more complex vocabulary. **This expansion is not meant to increase creativity but to produce a more specific explanation of a concept.**

5. Students save the edited organizer in the appropriate folder or directory.

6. Teachers assess the sentences for structure, variation, the use of transition words, and proper syntax to give feedback to the students. Secure that syntax, grammar, structure, and spelling are correct, students move to the formatting step.

The Formatting Step

In this step, students remove the structure words from the organizer and put the sentences into paragraph form as a draft.

1. Students highlight the structure words and colons and delete them. As each structure word is deleted, students sequence the sentences one after the other paying attention to beginning capitalization, ending punctuation, and spacing between sentences and lines.

2. Under "name," students add the day's date and any other information that belongs in the heading.

3. Students center the title and check words for proper capitalization.

4. Students indent the topic sentence.

5. Students read and listen again to the paragraph as a whole, assessing the flow and continuity of their paragraphs and making sure the order of the compared items is consistent.

Compare Paragraph Organizer by: Student

Title: Motorcycles and Bicycles
Topic Sentence: There are many similarities between motorcycles and bicycles.
Point of Comparison 1: Both motorcycles and bicycles have two wheels.
Detail Point 1A: Motorcycles have wide, rubber tires on their two wheels.
Detail Point 1B: Bicycles have two lighter and narrower rubber tires.
Point of Comparison 2: Likewise, motorcycles and bicycles have handlebars for steering.
Detail Point 2A: Motorcycle handlebars have a clutch on them.
Detail Point 2B: Many bicycle handlebars also have the gear controls on them.
Point of Comparison 3: Another likeness is that helmets are required for motorcycle and bicycle riders.
Detail Point 3A: All motorcycle riders are required by law to wear helmets in California.
Detail Point 3B: Children are required by law to wear helmets, and many adults also wear them for safety.
Concluding Sentence: Motorcycles and bicycles have many things in common.

Student
Date

Motorcycles and Bicycles

There are many similarities between motorcycles and bicycles. Both motorcycles and bicycles have two wheels. Motorcycles have wide, rubber tires on their two wheels. Bicycles have two lighter and narrower rubber tires. Likewise, motorcycles and bicycles have handlebars for steering. Motorcycle handlebars have a clutch on them. Many bicycle handlebars also have the gear controls on them. Another likeness is that helmets are required for motorcycle and bicycle riders. All motorcycle riders are required by law to wear helmets in California. Children are required by law to wear helmets, and many adults also wear them for safety. Motorcycles and bicycles have many things in common.

6. Students save the document as *'draft'* in the proper folder or directory and print it out in color, providing a copy to a proofreader to edit.

The Publishing Step

At this point, when students receive approved drafts, the writing process is completed except for removing the color and printing a final copy.

1. Students change the text color to black.
2. Students save the file in the appropriate folder or directory as *'final copy'* and print a final copy in black.
3. Students submit a complete packet containing the outline, organizer, draft, and final copy.

Once completed, the Compare Paragraph equates two items or ideas in order, with regard to three, clearly distinguished points, ending with a judgment about the comparison.

The Structured Writing Contrast Paragraph Process

After students have practiced writing Compare Paragraphs, teach the same paragraph structure using points of **contrast** between the same two items. The purpose of the Contrast Paragraph is to specifically examine the **differences** between two items.

The Planning Step

Students begin the planning step using an Inspiration template with the color-coded Compare and Contrast Paragraph web to organize their thoughts for writing. The color code and the text help identify the essential elements of the paragraph: title, topic sentence, three supporting **points of contrast**, two details elaborating the point of contrast for each of the items in order, and a conclusion.

Model the lesson by assigning a contrast paragraph on the topic **"Motorcycles Versus Bicycles."**

1. The white box in the web indidcates a place for the student's name, the blue box is for the paragraph title, and the yellow boxes are for the topic and concluding ideas. **The horizontal green box indicates Item A and Item B for the place and order of the two items to be contrasted. Item A will always be referred to before Item B in the supporting sentences.** The center vertical positioning of each point of contrast (structure sentences-green) allows for two sides of details. The red boxes hold the elaborating details for each item.

2. Students keyboard only single words and short phrases in the web to represent these contrasts. **Reinforce the concept of outlining as idea organization, not sentence writing.** The words and phrases will be converted into an outline to use as a guide for writing sentences in the organizer during the writing step of this process.

3. Students convert the web into a color-coded outline by selecting the outline

---

Contrast Paragraph Outline by:

I. Title:
    A. Topic Sentence:
    Points of Comparison
    Item A: Versus   Item B:
        1. Point 1:
            a. Detail Point 1A:
            b. Detail Point 1B:
        2. Point 2:
            a. Detail Point 2A:
            b. Detail Point 2B:
        3. Point 3:
            a. Detail Point 3A:
            b. Detail Point 3B:
    B. Concluding Sentence:

Contrast Paragraph Organizer by:

Title:
Topic Sentence:
Point of Comparison 1:
Detail Point 1A:
Detail Point 1B:
Point of Comparison 2:
Detail Point 2A:
Detail Point 2B:
Point of Comparison 3:
Detail Point 3A:
Detail Point 3B:
Concluding Sentence:

Chapter 8—The Compare and Contrast Paragraph Lesson

option in Inspiration and running spell check to make initial spelling corrections. Inspiration's spell checker can be difficult for some students to use. If this problem arises, defer spell checking to the first editing step. Students save their outlines in the appropriate folder or directory.

4. Students print the color-coded outline and give it to the teacher who checks the content and gives the students feedback. Reassured that the content is appropriate, the students use this outline to continue with the next step of the writing process, the writing step.

The Writing Step

Students use the color-coded Structured Writing **Compare and Contrast Paragraph Organizer** and a word-processing program (Write:Outloud) to guide and expand their ideas from the outline into complete sentences in the organizer, one at a time.

1. Using the outline as a guide, students write complete sentences in the orga-

nizer, one at a time. Each sentence will be revised and edited in the editing step, sentence by sentence.

2. Students expand and elaborate their sentences as they write. Teachers direct students to **use adjectives, adverbs, and prepositional phrases** to expand and clarify their writing, and to combine simple sentences into compound sentences.

3. Teachers should focus on two new concepts while teaching the Contrast Paragraph:

   • First, **points of contrast are the supporting sentences.** To make the detailed explanation clear, students identify these supporting points of contrast by adding specific **transition words** to direct the reader toward them. Teachers alert students to the different transition words they can use. Posting these examples helps students use transition words with confidence.

   • Second, **the details elaborate the points of contrast for each item in a specific order.** Each detail sentence

---

Contrast Paragraph Outline by: Student

I. Title: Motorcycles Versus Bicycles
    A. Topic Sentence: differences
    Points of Comparison (similarity or difference between the items)
    Item A : Motorcycles   **Versus**   **Item B:** Bicycles
        1. Point 1: power source
            a. Detail Point 1A: motor
            b. Detail Point 1B: pedals
        2. Point 2: license
            a. Detail Point 2A: required
            b. Detail Point 2B: not required
        3. Point 3: speed
            a. Detail Point 3A: fast
            b. Detail Point 3B: slow
    B. Concluding Sentence: very different vehicles

Contrast Paragraph Example

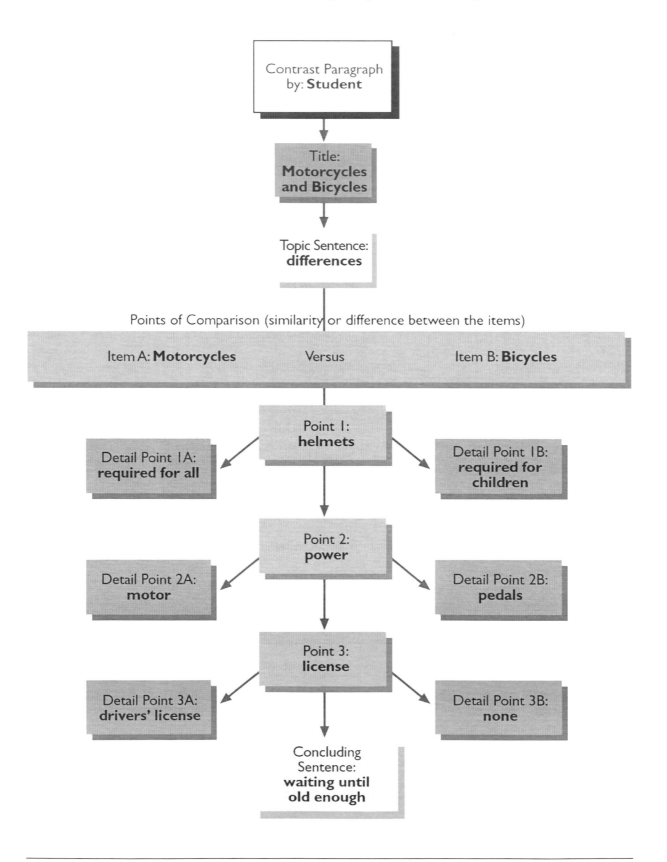

Contrast Paragraph
by: **Student**

Title:
**Motorcycles
and Bicycles**

Topic Sentence:
differences

Points of Comparison (similarity or difference between the items)

Item A: **Motorcycles**   Versus   Item B: **Bicycles**

Point 1:
helmets

Detail Point 1A:
required for all

Detail Point 1B:
**required for
children**

Point 2:
power

Detail Point 2A:
motor

Detail Point 2B:
pedals

Point 3:
license

Detail Point 3A:
drivers' license

Detail Point 3B:
none

Concluding
Sentence:
**waiting until
old enough**

explains the item (A, then B) with regard to the point of contrast.

4. Once all the sentences are completed, the students save the organizer in the proper folder or directory.

5. At this point, the teacher assesses the document for sentence structure and suggests expanding terms when appropriate.

The Editing Step

Students are required to use a specific editing process to make sure their sentences reflect what they mean to convey and to correct spelling and mechanical errors. This step becomes more complex as the students proceed through the Structured Writing sequence.

1. Students use text-to-speech to read and listen to each sentence, one at a time. Here, students add, delete, and change words until the sentences sound right and communicate what they mean.

2. Students check capitalization (the beginning of each sentence and proper nouns) and punctuation, word usage, and spelling. We recommend that students be taught to do this editing in the specific order. Using the spell checker in the word processor as the last step gives students a better chance to properly correct misspelled words.

3. Students make sure that **three points of contrast** support the topic sentence, and that appropriate transition words indicate each point of contrast. Students check to ensure details elaborate each specific point of contrast in the proper order.

4. During editing, after the initial structure, sequence, and purpose have been set, students revise sentences to refine the paragraph. These skills are taught only when the students are secure in their ability to clearly write a Contrast

---

Contrast Paragraph Organizer by: Student

Title: Motorcycles Versus Bicycles
Topic Sentence: There are many differences between motorcycles and bicycles.
Point of Comparison 1: The most obvious difference between motorcycles and bicycles is the power source.
Detail Point 1A: Motorcycles have a motor to power them.
Detail Point 1B: Bicycles have pedals that are pushed by a person's feet to provide their power.
Point of Comparison 2: Unlike motorcycle riders, bicycle riders are not required to have a driver's license.
Detail Point 2A: Motorcycle riders are required to have a valid driver's license to drive their vehicles legally.
Detail Point 2B: Bicycle riders, on the other hand, can be very young children who are not required to have any kind of license to ride their bikes.
Point of Comparison 3: Another difference between motorcycles and bicycles is the speed that they can go.
Detail Point 3A: Motorcycles go very fast because they are powered by gasoline motors.
Detail Point 3B: Bicycles go much slower than motorcycles because they only have human legs to power them.
Concluding Sentence: Motorcycles and bicycles are distinctly different vehicles.

Paragraph. Students need to **vary the structure of their sentences** (imperative, declarative, interrogatory, exclamatory), and **use the thesaurus** to develop a more complex vocabulary. **This expansion is not meant to increase creativity but to produce a more specific explanation of a concept.**

5. Students save the edited organizer in the proper folder or directory.

6. Teachers assess the sentences for structure, variation, the use of transition words, and proper syntax to give feedback to the students. Secure that syntax, grammar, structure, and spelling are correct, students move to the formatting step.

The formatting and publishing steps remain the same for the various Compare and Contrast Paragraph types.

Student
Date

Motorcycles Versus Bicycles

There are many differences between motorcycles and bicycles. The most obvious difference between motorcycles and bicycles is the power source. Motorcycles have a motor to power them. Bicycles have pedals that are pushed by a person's feet to provide their power. Unlike motorcycle riders, bicycle riders are not required to have a driver's license. Motorcycle riders are required to have a valid driver's license to drive their vehicles legally. Bicycle riders, on the other hand, can be very young children who are not required to have any kind of license to ride their bikes. Another difference between motorcycles and bicycles is the speed that they can go. Motorcycles go very fast because they are powered by gasoline motors. Bicycles go much slower than motorcycles because they only have human legs to power them. Motorcycles and bicycles are distinctly different vehicles.

The *Structured Writing* Compare and Contrast Paragraph Process

When the students have practiced writing Compare Paragraphs and Contrast Paragraphs, explore a paragraph that mixes both comparison and contrasting points. Following the topic of **Motorcycles Versus Bicycles**, the points might be a mixture of those used in the first two Compare and Contrast Paragraphs. On the next page is an example of this strategy.

In summary, the Structured Writing Compare and Contrast Paragraph uses:

♦ Two objects or ideas as the central subject of the paragraph

♦ Points of comparison or contrast between the two objects or ideas as the supporting sentences

♦ Transition words to identify the points of comparison and contrast

♦ Details to elaborate the points of comparison and contrast

♦ Two objects/ideas in specific order

Compare and Contrast Paragraph Example

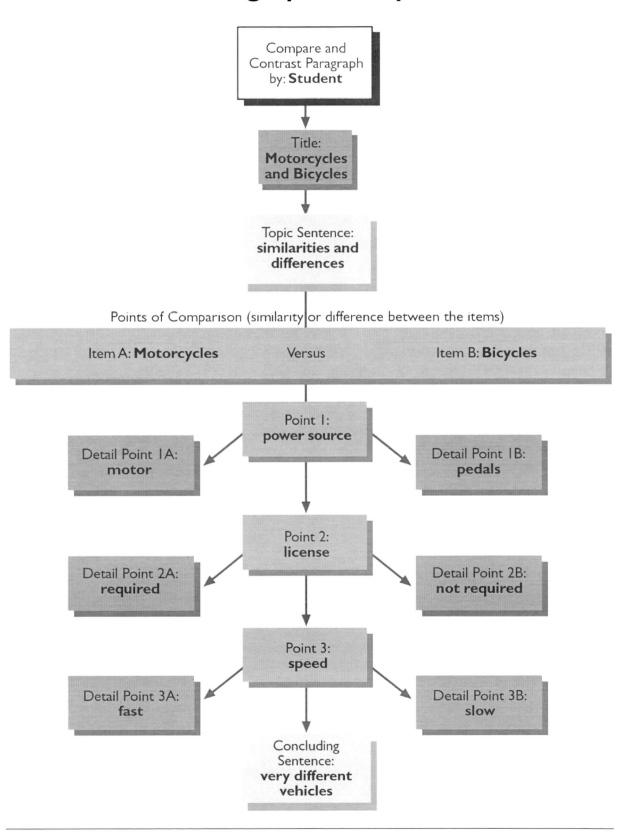

Compare and Contrast Paragraph by: **Student**

Title: **Motorcycles and Bicycles**

Topic Sentence: **similarities and differences**

Points of Comparison (similarity or difference between the items)

Item A: **Motorcycles**   Versus   Item B: **Bicycles**

Point 1: **power source**

Detail Point 1A: **motor**   Detail Point 1B: **pedals**

Point 2: **license**

Detail Point 2A: **required**   Detail Point 2B: **not required**

Point 3: **speed**

Detail Point 3A: **fast**   Detail Point 3B: **slow**

Concluding Sentence: **very different vehicles**

Compare and Contrast Paragraph Outline by: Student

I. Title: Motorcycles Versus Bicycles
    A. Topic Sentence: many similarities and differences
    Points of Comparison (similarity or difference between the items)
    Item A: Motorcycles   **Versus**   **Item B:** Bicycles
        1. Point 1: helmets
            a. Detail Point 1A: required for all
            b. Detail Point 1B: required for children
        2. Point 2: power source
            a. Detail Point 2A: motor
            b. Detail Point 2B: pedals
        3. Point 3: license
            a. Detail Point 3B: drivers' license required
            b. Detail Point 3A: none required
    B. Concluding Sentence: waiting until old enough

Students use the same writing sequence for all paragraph types. Only the content and structure varies. This repetition develops a natural flow in writing which can be hard for many students to achieve. Using the computer reduces the task load and allows for easy multiple editing in order to achieve more complex, error-free documents.

Compare and Contrast Paragraph Organizer by: Student

Title: Motorcycles Versus Bicycles
Topic Sentence: There are many similarities and differences between motorcycles and bicycles.
Point of Comparison 1: Both motorcycle riders and bicycle riders are required to wear helmets.
Detail Point 1A: All motorcycle riders are required by law to wear helmets in California.
Detail Point 1B: California law requires all children to wear helmets while riding bikes.
Point of Comparison 2: On the other hand, the power source of the two vehicles is quite different
Detail Point 2A: Motorcycles have a motor to power them and can attain very high speeds.
Detail Point 2B: Bicycles have pedals that are pushed by a person's feet to provide their power, so they go much slower than motorcycles.
Point of Comparison 3: Another difference between motorcycles and bicycles is the licensing of the riders.
Detail Point 3A: Motorcycle riders are required to have a valid driver's license to drive motorcycles legally.
Detail Point 3B: Bicycle riders, on the other hand, can be very young children who are not required to have any kind of license to ride their bikes.
Concluding Sentence: I really enjoy riding my bicycle now, but I can't wait until I am old enough to ride a motorcycle!

Student
Date

Motorcycles Versus Bicycles

There are many similarities and differences between motorcycles and bicycles. Both motorcycle riders and bicycle riders are required to wear helmets. All motorcycle riders are required by law to wear helmets in California. California law requires all children to wear helmets while riding bikes. On the other hand, the power source of the two vehicles is quite different. Motorcycles have a motor to power them and can attain very high speeds. Bicycles have pedals that are pushed by a person's feet to provide their power, so they go much slower than motorcycles. Another difference between motorcycles and bicycles is the licensing of the riders. Motorcycle riders are required to have a valid driver's license to drive motorcycles legally. Bicycle riders, on the other hand, can be very young children who are not required to have any kind of license to ride their bikes. I really enjoy riding my bicycle now, but I can't wait until I am old enough to ride a motorcycle!

Suggested Topics for Compare and Contrast Paragraphs

- Two schools, two cars, two teachers, two pets, two friends
- Two sports, two video games, two vehicles
- Computer versus pencil
- Movies versus live theater
- School uniforms versus no uniforms

Conclusion

Many students do not have sufficient background information or experience to begin the arduous task of writing paragraphs. Having spent little productive time with the written word, it is difficult for them to intuitively understand the structure expected in written language. It has been shown that a specific, direct instruction method is the most likely path of success for students having difficulty with writing.

Also, we have found that many students work better with a graphic, global view rather than the verbal, linear approach most often used to teach writing. The Structured Writing technique using matched templates from Inspiration and an organizer in a word-processing program (Write: OutLoud) provides that graphic view, gives specific direct instruction, and allows for the linear conversion necessary to complete an acceptable paragraph.

During the instruction sequence, the writing process remains virtually the same. However, the structure required within each paragraph varies with the paragraph type. Each paragraph builds on the previously learned one and the complexity increases. The steps in the **Structured Writing** process are:

- ◆ **Planning step:** Uses an Inspiration web template to organize ideas and generate an outline to guide writing.

- ◆ **Writing step:** A word-processing organizer (Write:OutLoud) is color coded to match the Inspiration outline and allows students to expand and organize their ideas into a paragraph, one sentence at a time.

- ◆ **Editing/Revising step:** Using the editing functions of a word-processing program, the students correct capitalization, punctuation, and spelling errors. The students expands their sentences using modifiers, adjectives, adverbs, and prepositional phrases. Students vary sentence structure and enhance vocabulary using the thesaurus.

- ◆ **Formatting step:** The structure words are removed from the document and sentences are placed into paragraph or draft form. Students reread their work to ensure that they have used proper transition words to identify the supporting sentences.

- ◆ **Publishing step:** After approval of a proofreader, the document is corrected, the color code is removed from the corrected document, and the paragraph is published as a final copy.

As the structure varies in the specific paragraphs, students learn to visually recognize the various paragraph types. They learn to recognize the structured webs and understand what types of supporting sentences are appropriate. The ability to differentiate between various paragraph types helps students determine the type of paragraph needed to best expand a concept or to answer a question in writing.

Experience with the structured paragraph writing process is critical for preparing students to be proficient writers. When the structure is mastered, students become more creative in their writing.

The Structured Writing process can be expanded to introduce multiple paragraph writing (use the **Essay** template available on the accompanying CD-ROM). Again, the built-in structure of the writing process guides the students to early success. As the instructor, you can adapt this process to essays, book reports, research reports or any other type of writing assignment.

Appendix

National Educational Technology Standards (NETS) and Performance Indicators for Students

The National Educational Technology Standards for Students are divided into six broad categories. Standards within each category are to be introduced, reinforced, and mastered by students. These categories provide a framework for linking performance indicators, listed by grade level, to the standards. Teachers can use these standards and profiles as guidelines for planning technology-based activities in which students achieve success in learning, communication, and life skills.

1. **Basic operations and concepts**
   - Students demonstrate a sound understanding of the nature and operation of technology systems.
   - Students are proficient in the use of technology.

2. **Social, ethical, and human issues**
   - Students understand the ethical, cultural, and societal issues related to technology.
   - Students practice responsible use of technology systems, information, and software.
   - Students develop positive attitudes toward technology uses that support lifelong learning, collaboration, personal pursuits, and productivity.

3. **Technology productivity tools**
   - Students use technology tools to enhance learning, increase productivity, and promote creativity.
   - Students use productivity tools to collaborate in constructing technology-enhanced models, preparing publications, and producing other creative works.

4. **Technology communications tools**
   - Students use telecommunications to collaborate, publish, and interact with peers, experts, and other audiences.
   - Students use a variety of media and formats to communicate information and ideas effectively to multiple audiences.

5. **Technology research tools**
   - Students use technology to locate, evaluate, and collect information from a variety of sources.
   - Students use technology tools to process data and report results.
   - Students evaluate and select new information resources and technological innovations based on the appropriateness to specific tasks.

6. **Technology problem-solving and decision-making tools**
   - Students use technology resources for solving problems and making informed decisions.
   - Students employ technology in the development of strategies for solving problems in the real world.

Performance Indicators for Technology-Literate Students

All students should have opportunities to demonstrate the following performances. Numbers in parentheses following each performance indicator refer to the standards category to which the performance is linked.

Grades PreK–2

Prior to completion of Grade 2, students will:

1. Use input devices (e.g., mouse, keyboard, remote control) and output devices (e.g., monitor, printer) to successfully operate computers, VCRs, audio-tapes, and other technologies. (1)

2. Use a variety of media and technology resources for directed and independent learning activities. (1, 3)

3. Communicate about technology using developmentally appropriate and accurate terminology. (1)

4. Use developmentally appropriate multimedia resources (e.g., interactive books, educational software, elementary multimedia encyclopedias) to support learning. (1)

5. Work cooperatively and collaboratively with peers, family members, and others when using technology in the classroom. (2)

6. Demonstrate positive social and ethical behaviors when using technology. (2)

7. Practice responsible use of technology systems and software. (2)

8. Create developmentally appropriate multimedia products with support from teachers, family members, or student partners. (3)

9. Use technology resources (e.g., puzzles, logical thinking programs, writing tools, digital cameras, drawing tools) for problem solving, communication, and illustration of thoughts, ideas, and stories. (3, 4, 5, 6)

10. Gather information and communicate with others using telecommunications, with support from teachers, family members, or student partners. (4)

Grades 3–5

Prior to completion of Grade 5, students will:

1. Use keyboards and other common input and output devices (including adaptive devices when necessary) efficiently and effectively. (1)

2. Discuss common uses of technology in daily life and the advantages and disadvantages those uses provide. (1, 2)

3. Discuss basic issues related to responsible use of technology and information and describe personal consequences of inappropriate use. (2)

4. Use general purpose productivity tools and peripherals to support personal productivity, remediate skill deficits, and facilitate learning throughout the curriculum. (3)

5. Use technology tools (e.g., multimedia authoring, presentation, Web tools, digital cameras, scanners) for individual and collaborative writing, communication, and publishing activities to create knowledge products for audiences inside and outside the classroom. (3, 4)

6. Use telecommunications efficiently and effectively to access remote information, communicate with others in support of direct and independent learning, and pursue personal interests. (4)

7. Use telecommunications and online resources (e.g., e-mail, online discussions, Web environments) to participate in collaborative problem-solving activities for the purpose of developing solutions or products for audiences inside and outside the classroom. (4, 5)

8. Use technology resources (e.g., calculators, data collection probes, videos, educational software) for problem-solving, self-directed learning, and extended learning activities. (5, 6)

9. Determine when technology is useful and select the appropriate tool(s) and technology resources to address a variety of tasks and problems. (5, 6)

10. Evaluate the accuracy, relevance, appropriateness, comprehensiveness, and bias of electronic information sources. (6)

Grades 6–8

Prior to completion of Grade 8, students will:

1. Apply strategies for identifying and solving routine hardware and software problems that occur during everyday use. (1)

2. Demonstrate knowledge of current changes in information technologies and the effect those changes have on the workplace and society. (2)

3. Exhibit legal and ethical behaviors when using information and technology, and discuss consequences of misuse. (2)

4. Use content-specific tools, software, and simulations (e.g., environmental probes, graphing calculators, exploratory environments, Web tools) to support learning and research. (3, 5)

5. Apply productivity/multimedia tools and peripherals to support personal productivity, group collaboration, and learning throughout the curriculum. (3, 6)

6. Design, develop, publish, and present products (e.g., Web pages, videotapes) using technology resources that demonstrate and communicate curriculum concepts to audiences inside and outside the classroom. (4, 5, 6)

7. Collaborate with peers, experts, and others using telecommunications and collaborative tools to investigate curriculum-related problems, issues, and information, and to develop solutions or products for audiences inside and outside the classroom. (4, 5)

8. Select and use appropriate tools and technology resources to accomplish a variety of tasks and solve problems. (5, 6)

9. Demonstrate an understanding of concepts underlying hardware, software, and connectivity, and of practical applications to learning and problem solving. (1, 6)

10. Research and evaluate the accuracy, relevance, appropriateness, comprehensiveness, and bias of electronic information sources concerning real-world problems. (2, 5, 6)

Grades 9–12

Prior to completion of Grade 12, students will:

1. Identify capabilities and limitations of contemporary and emerging technology resources and assess the potential of these systems and services to address personal, lifelong learning, and workplace needs. (2)

2. Make informed choices among technology systems, resources, and services. (1, 2)

3. Analyze advantages and disadvantages of widespread use and reliance on technology in the workplace and in society as a whole. (2)

4. Demonstrate and advocate for legal and ethical behavior among peers, family, and community regarding the use of technology and information. (2)

5. Use technology tools and resources for managing and communicating personal/professional information (e.g., finances, schedules, addresses, purchases, correspondence). (3, 4)

6. Evaluate technology-based options, including distance and distributed education, for lifelong learning. (5)

7. Routinely and efficiently use online information resources to meet needs for collaboration, research, publications, communications, and productivity. (4, 5, 6)

8. Select and apply technology tools for research, information analysis, problem-solving, and decision-making in content learning. (4, 5)

9. Investigate and apply expert systems, intelligent agents, and simulations in real-world situations. (3, 5, 6)

10. Collaborate with peers, experts, and others to contribute a content-related knowledge base by using technology to compile, synthesize, produce, and disseminate information, models, and other creative works. (4, 5, 6)

National Educational Technology Standards (NETS) and Performance Indicators for Teachers

All classroom teachers should be prepared to meet the following standards and performance indicators.

I. Technology Operations and Concepts

Teachers demonstrate a sound understanding of technology operations and concepts. Teachers:

A. demonstrate introductory knowledge, skills, and understanding of concepts related to technology (as described in the ISTE National Educational Technology Standards for Students).

B. demonstrate continual growth in technology knowledge and skills to stay abreast of current and emerging technologies.

II. Planning and Designing Learning Environments and Experiences

Teachers plan and design effective learning environments and experiences supported by technology. Teachers:

A. design developmentally appropriate learning opportunities that apply technology-enhanced instructional strategies to support the diverse needs of learners.

B. apply current research on teaching and learning with technology when planning learning environments and experiences.

C. identify and locate technology resources and evaluate them for accuracy and suitability.

D. plan for the management of technology resources within the context of learning activities.

E. plan strategies to manage student learning in a technology-enhanced environment.

III. Teaching, Learning, and the Curriculum

Teachers implement curriculum plans that include methods and strategies for applying technology to maximize student learning. Teachers:

A. facilitate technology-enhanced experiences that address content standards and student technology standards.

B. use technology to support learner-centered strategies that address the diverse needs of students.

C. apply technology to develop students' higher-order skills and creativity.

D. manage student learning activities in a technology-enhanced environment.

IV. Assessment and Evaluation

Teachers apply technology to facilitate a variety of effective assessment and evaluation strategies. Teachers:

A. apply technology in assessing student learning of subject matter using a variety of assessment techniques.

B. use technology resources to collect and analyze data, interpret results, and communicate findings to improve instructional practice and maximize student learning.

C. apply multiple methods of evaluation to determine students' appropriate use of technology resources for learning, communication, and productivity.

V. Productivity and Professional Practice

Teachers use technology to enhance their productivity and professional practice. Teachers:

A. use technology resources to engage in ongoing professional development and lifelong learning.

B. continually evaluate and reflect on professional practice to make informed decisions regarding the use of technology in support of student learning.

C. apply technology to increase productivity.

D. use technology to communicate and collaborate with peers, parents, and the larger community in order to nurture student learning.

VI. Social, Ethical, Legal, and Human Issues

Teachers understand the social, ethical, legal, and human issues surrounding the use of technology in PK–12 schools and apply that understanding in practice. Teachers:

A. model and teach legal and ethical practice related to technology use.

B. apply technology resources to enable and empower learners with diverse backgrounds, characteristics, and abilities.

C. identify and use technology resources that affirm diversity.

D. promote safe and healthy use of technology resources.

E. facilitate equitable access to technology resources for all students.